GROUND FORCE
GARDEN HANDBOOK

GROUND FORCE GARDEN HANDBOOK

Alan Titchmarsh,
Charlie Dimmock
and Tommy Walsh

with Sue Fisher

This book is published to accompany the television series entitled *Ground Force,* which was first broadcast in 1997. The series was produced by Bazal (part of ENDEMOL Entertainment UK) for BBC Television.

Executive Producer: Carol Haslam
Producer/director: John Thornicroft

Published by BBC Worldwide Limited, Woodlands,
80 Wood Lane, London W12 0TT

First published 2001
This edition published in 2001 for AMS
Copyright © Alan Titchmarsh,
Charlie Dimmock and Tommy Walsh 2001
The moral right of the authors has been asserted.

ISBN 0 563 53449 4

Commissioning Editor: Nicky Copeland
Project Editor: Rachel Copus
Designer: Isobel Gillan
Illustrator: Amanda Patton
Picture Researcher: Bea Thomas

Set in Helvetica Neue
Printed and bound by Imprimerie
Pollina s.a. - n° L82184
Colour origination by Imprimerie
Pollina s.a.
Jacket printed by Imprimerie
Pollina s.a.

CONTENTS

Introduction

A garden created by the *Ground Force* team can be a dream come true, and one you've made yourself can be almost as good. But once the dust has settled and the concrete has set on your newly made-over plot, what then? Gardens are full of living, ever-changing plants, plus features and structures, all of which are bound to need a bit of care over time – something occasionally overlooked by some owners of *Ground Force* gardens who have been surprised and not a little embarrassed by the team's unexpected return visit a year later.

Keeping your plot in good shape need not be hard work, and caring for your garden can be a hugely enjoyable experience, as well as providing a supremely effective way of winding down after a hectic day at work or looking after a family. Routine jobs like weeding, cutting the grass, and pruning and training plants are easy if done on a regular basis. Ignore your garden at your peril, though, for during the growing season it can very quickly get out of hand – as anyone who has returned from a fortnight's summer holiday is only too well aware!

First-time gardeners may understandably feel a bit confused about the whole business. A visit to the garden centre reveals more plants and products than you'd ever thought existed and, as is always the way, just about all the other customers seem to know exactly what they need – or at least, look as though they do. And as if that wasn't enough, during the busy spring and summer months when your garden is crying out for attention garden centres will be absolutely packed, with knowledgeable members of staff in very short supply indeed. What you really need is the *Ground Force* team on hand all the time, with their friendly, helpful and no-nonsense approach that takes the mystery out of gardening. While you can't have them in person, this book is the next best thing.

The first chapter starts with the very basics of looking after a garden: what equipment and products will be needed, how to look after your plants and why these basic jobs like watering, feeding, weeding and pruning actually need doing at all. Getting all these jobs done with the minimum of work is a theme that runs right through the book, as few of us are lucky enough to have unlimited time at our disposal. Of course, not everyone can keep on top of things all the time, so if you have visitors coming or just want to get your garden into shape quickly, turn to 'A quick tidy-up' on page 36. Then, venture into the realms of making a permanent change for the better with some of the ideas from 'Half-day jobs' on page 38 or the following section 'Weekend transformations'.

The next chapter, 'Plants and planting', describes some of the many hundreds of plants that are available – from trees and shrubs to bulbs and biennials, roses and perennials – and tells you how to plant and care for them. Container gardening is one of the easiest ways of adding colour and interest to a garden throughout the year and the results can be sensational. Chapter three, 'Container gardening' gives you the lowdown on how to achieve this in a variety of pot gardens, including low-maintenance containers and those with an edible theme. In chapter four, 'Water gardening' we look at how to maintain ponds, fountains and waterfalls and the plants that thrive in them, and there is also heaps of useful information on caring for fish and the wildlife that the features attract. The next chapter, 'Garden features' describes eye-catching structures ranging from arches and pergolas to fences and buildings like summerhouses and gazebos, as well as 'accessories' like furniture and barbecues. Finally, 'Jobs for the month' lists the tasks that will keep everything flourishing – and put the *Ground Force* stamp on your garden.

THE GROUND RULES

The right tools for the job

Like most things in life, you get what you pay for, and gardening tools are a shining example of this. All the basic equipment is likely to see lots of use and so it's well worth buying more expensive tools that will last for many years, rather than cheap ones which tend to cost more in the long run because they need to be replaced frequently. Another bonus is that good quality tools are often easier to use. Garden tools make excellent presents so drop a few hints around Christmas and birthdays, then hopefully you will receive something much more useful than bath salts and ill-fitting jumpers!

The following list covers all the tools you'll need for basic planting, soil preparation and garden care, including weed control and pruning. Equipment for lawns is on pages 32–3.

Fork Buy a full-width fork for digging over the ground, making planting holes and moving bulky materials. A narrower one is good if you just want to lightly dig the soil between existing plants. Forks come with handles of varying lengths so choose one to suit your height.

Spade Use for the same jobs as a fork. It's possible to manage without a spade on heavy soils, but not if you garden on light, sandy or stony soil as this will run through the tines or prongs of a fork. A spade is also good for moving finer materials like mulch.

Rake For levelling soil and breaking down the lumpy surface ready for planting or seed sowing. Don't confuse a garden rake with a lawn rake (page 30).

Hoe Unless your garden is really tiny, do invest in a hoe – it's great for keeping on top of weeds and will save lots of wear and tear on your back. A Dutch hoe is the best type for general weeding.

Trowel For planting and weeding. It will see loads of use, so don't even consider buying a cheap one.

Shears A standard short-handled pair will do duty for lots of jobs such as trimming hedges, shrubs and perennials as well as lawn edges.

Basic gardening equipment will see a lot of use, so it's worth buying good quality tools wherever possible.

Secateurs that are clean and sharp will be a pleasure to use.

Secateurs Invaluable for pruning, trimming and deadheading. The main choice is between anvil-type secateurs and ones with 'parrot-bill' shaped blades. Choose the parrot-bill type if you're likely to be doing lots of pruning. Secateurs are easy to lose, so it's well worth also buying a belt holster.

Watering can Metal cans are long-lasting but plastic ones are quite a bit cheaper. Buy a full-size, long-spouted can unless lifting it when it's full will be a problem. Use a large plastic drinks bottle to reach up and water hanging baskets, instead of buying another, smaller can.

Wheelbarrow or bucket/carrying bag For moving rubbish and materials. If your garden is large you'll need to use a wheelbarrow, but in a small plot it's possible to manage with a builders' bucket or a stout plastic carrying bag designed for garden use. If a wheelbarrow is likely to see lots of heavy use like shifting rubble, buy a large, strong model from a builders' supplier rather than a lightweight garden barrow.

how to make a tool rack

1 Cut two pieces of 25 × 50mm (1 × 2in) timber to the required length. Nail one length in position about 1.2m (4ft) from the ground, and the other one about 1.8m (6ft) from the ground.

2 Hammer two 10cm (4in) nails into the top length of timber for the fork, and two for the spade. Position them either so that the handle of the tool can be hooked over both nails, or slotted between them.

3 Fix a narrow shelf over the top of the rack for storing fiddly items like garden twine, containers of fertilizer and so on.

Improving your soil

One of the most confusing sights down at the garden centre, nursery or DIY store is all those vast stacks of bulky, multicoloured bags. There are potting composts and planting composts, concentrated manures and mulches, with or without lime – it's bewilderment in a bag. So here is an at-a-glance guide to what they all do and which ones you're likely to need.

SOIL IMPROVERS

Soil improvers should be used when you are preparing ground for planting. They consist of bulky, well-rotted organic matter that will improve all types of soil by giving them a greater capacity for holding on to the water and food your plants need, as well as making a better environment for roots to grow in. Materials available in bags are composted bark, composted straw and concentrated animal manure. Avoid peat, which is a non-renewable resource.

Unless your garden is small, buying enough packaged soil conditioner will be expensive. Look for cheaper alternatives like horse or farmyard manure, spent mushroom compost and spent hops, all of which are often advertised on local notice boards and in newspapers. Manure should be at least six months old if you're planning to plant in the near future.

For details on making your own soil improver by recycling garden and kitchen waste and instructions on adding organic matter to your soil, see pages 14–15.

PLANTING COMPOST

Planting compost is designed to give plants a really good start in life – which is very important with long-lived permanent ones like trees, shrubs, climbers, roses and perennials. The compost is made up of a

Cover bare soil with a mulch to improve plant growth and to cut down on the amount of weeding you'll need to do.

fine grade of organic matter, plus fertilizer to feed the plant for its first season, and often contains water-retaining granules that provide a reservoir of moisture during dry spells. When planting, mix a couple of forkfuls into the planting hole and into the soil that has been dug out ready for backfilling.

MULCHES

A mulch is a layer of material that is put on the bare soil between plants. It improves plant growth and also cuts down on your work – which can't be bad! It reduces the amount of water that evaporates from the soil, stops the vast majority of weeds from growing and also helps to prevent plant roots from becoming too hot or too cold.

Chipped bark and cocoa shell are the most popular materials. Mulch only when the soil is wet, and spread a layer of material 5–10cm (2–4in) thick over the bare soil between plants. Top up the mulch every spring as the material will break down slowly over time, helping to improve the condition of the soil. Put upturned pots or buckets over small plants. This will prevent the mulch getting into their centres and possibly causing rotting.

POTTING COMPOSTS

All plants in containers need to be grown in potting compost because they need to get their roots into something really good in order to grow well in such confined spaces. Whatever you do, don't be tempted to eke out your potting compost with a cheaper soil improver or garden soil – the poor results just aren't worth it.

The main choice is between soil-based or soil-less composts. Those based on soil (often referred to as loam) are dense and heavy, ideal for long-lived plants such as shrubs, perennials, grasses and roses. The main exception is if any of these plants will be in places where weight is an issue, such as hanging baskets, window boxes or roof gardens. If so, opt for soil-less compost which is usually based on composted bark or coir, and is much lighter. Short-lived seasonal plants like annuals, tender perennials and bulbs are best grown in this anyway, regardless of where you're planting.

Whatever your soil type, add lots of organic matter when preparing the ground.

Two popular types of compost are intended for specific plants or uses. Ericaceous or lime-free compost is essential for growing certain plants that hate lime, notably rhododendrons, azaleas, pieris and camellias. Seed and cuttings compost is a fine-textured compost formulated for propagation purposes. It contains little or no fertilizer as this can scorch or kill the delicate roots of young plants.

> ## buy in bulk and save money
>
> You will need lots of soil improvers and mulch if you're tackling a whole garden. Instead of buying lots of small bags, save money by buying a bulk load of material which will be delivered loose or in large, plain bags.

Recycling garden rubbish

Few things warm the cockles of a gardener's heart more than seeing plants bursting with health and covered in bloom. The answer really does lie in the soil, and the way to keep plants healthy is by regular additions of bulky soil improvers like those described on page 12. But instead of buying in all your requirements, you can save yourself money and improve your garden by composting garden rubbish and some from the kitchen as well. Most waste can be turned into compost and you'll do the environment a good turn by saving on the amount that goes into landfill sites.

Recycle garden rubbish to improve your soil – it'll save money and be good for the environment at the same time.

MAKING GARDEN COMPOST

Garden compost is great for conditioning the soil and helping to feed plants. The quickest way to make it is in a special bin. There are lots of different ready-made ones available – local councils often supply bins at bargain prices – or you can make a wooden one. Construct a metre-square cube with slotted planks on one side so that compost can be removed easily. Whichever option you go for, try to find room for two bins so that one can be 'cooking' while the other is being filled.

Start by spreading some woody prunings in the base of the bin. This will let air circulate through the heap. As the bin fills with waste, mix fine and coarse materials together and add a compost activator to speed the rotting process. Water if dry, and cover to keep rainwater out and heat in. If you're really enthusiastic and want perfect compost in the shortest possible time, empty the heap out after a month or two, give it a good mixing and chuck it back in for a few more weeks. However, left to its own devices your heap should still turn into dark, crumbly compost in about six to nine months.

Do put in Weeds, soft prunings, chopped or shredded woody stems, grass clippings, leaves, fresh horse or farmyard manure, uncooked vegetable waste, tea bags, scrunched-up newspaper and cardboard.

Don't put in Roots of perennial weeds, weed seeds, bits of diseased plants, dog or cat faeces.

SHREDDERS AND SHREDDING

A shredder is great for chopping up woody branches to use in compost or as a mulch. However, smaller models can be slow and tiresome to use, while larger ones are expensive. The answer is to hire a large shredder if you only need one occasionally. The cost can be reduced by clubbing together with a couple of neighbours. Remember to wear stout gloves and goggles when using the shredder, and take great care near moving parts.

making leaf mould

1 Rake up leaves within a few days of falling as they can smother grass and plants.

2 Polythene sacks are ideal for making leaf mould. Use a garden fork to pierce a few holes in the bag to let moisture out and air in.

3 Fill the sack, squashing down the leaves as you go. Tie the top and leave for at least a year before use.

ADDING ORGANIC MATTER TO YOUR SOIL

If you are creating a garden on new ground, or in a plot that has been neglected, it is vital to improve the soil by adding organic matter. Light, free-draining soils need this bulky material to improve their capacity to hold water and nutrients, while heavy soils such as clay need it to open out their soil structure and improve drainage.

In most cases it is sufficient to dig over the soil to one spade's depth, working in organic matter as you go. However, ground that is in poor condition or that has little topsoil, such as the garden of a new house, needs double digging. To do this, dig a trench to the depth of two spades and put the soil to one side. Using a fork, dig over the soil in the base of the trench as deeply as possible, working in organic matter. Do the same in a second, parallel trench and use the soil you remove from it to fill the first one. Work the whole area in this fashion, filling in the last trench with the soil from the first one.

Heavy soils are best dug in autumn and left rough in large clods. The winter frosts will help break them down.

Dig the ground thoroughly before planting, working in lots of organic matter. Single digging is usually sufficient but double digging is worth doing on new ground.

Feeding your plants

Plants need a regular supply of food in order to grow strong and healthy – not food of the steak-and-chips variety but invisible, water-soluble nutrients that are found in the soil. However, because gardening involves growing a lot of plants in a limited space, they take more out of the soil than goes back in naturally and will need feeding with fertilizer at least a couple of times a year.

So far, so good, but a trip to the garden centre will reveal a bewildering array of plant foods, in brightly coloured packaging and a whole range of forms, which broadly fall into one of the groups listed opposite. All these are general fertilizers – that is, they supply all the nutrients a plant should need. The main difference between them lies in how quickly the plant gets its food and how long the fertilizer's effect lasts.

It's important not to confuse fertilizers, which are plant foods in concentrated form, with soil improvers like manure and compost. The improvers do contain some nutrients, but not enough to keep your plants well fed.

The time to feed all established plants is in spring and summer when they're growing strongly. Only annuals should be fed after mid-summer, as late feeding of permanent plants encourages lots of soft, new growth that is easily damaged by frost. Plants can only take up fertilizer when the ground is damp, so don't bother applying it in dry weather. The best conditions for feeding are when the ground is moist but the plants are dry – fertilizer can stick to and scorch damp leaves. If you do get any fertilizer on to the plants themselves, brush it off and then water the plants.

Always follow the manufacturer's instructions when feeding. Don't fall into the common trap of putting on too much fertilizer on the basis that double the feed will do twice as much good – it doesn't! In fact, overfeeding can do plants more harm than giving them no food at all.

Right: Well-established garden plants should be fed every spring with slow-release or controlled-release fertilizer.

plant-specific fertilizers

Fertilizers that encourage specific plants to achieve their best performance can also be used for other plants.
- Tomato fertilizer is good for all fruiting plants.
- Lime-hating or ericaceous plants benefit from an ericaceous fertilizer.
- Rose fertilizer can be used for all flowering plants.

Organic fertilizers tend to be more beneficial to soils than inorganic chemicals.

type	how it works	what to feed and when
Planting fertilizer	Contains nutrients that boost root growth	All garden plants on planting. Bonemeal is for autumn or winter planting
Slow release	As the name suggests, the nutrients are released over a period of time	All garden plants, in early spring
Controlled release	'Smart' fertilizer; coated with temperature-sensitive resin, so nutrients are only released when plants are growing enough to need feeding	All garden plants, in spring. All containers. More expensive than slow-release but also much more effective
Liquid	Nutrients are immediately available to plants but don't remain effective for long, so frequent applications required	Container plants and any garden plants in need of a quick pick-me-up. Spring to late summer. Usually watered on to the soil but can also be sprayed on foliage for the very fastest results

All, apart from liquid fertilizer, should be lightly raked or hoed into the soil.

Weeds and weeding

Weeding is one of the downsides of gardening and something that most people hate with a passion. The trouble is, there's just no way of having a garden to enjoy without having to do at least a little bit of regular weed control. Weeds are immensely successful simply because they have evolved to grow best in your locality, so they'll nearly always be able to outperform garden plants.

However, it's not all doom and gloom. Bringing a weedy patch under control need not be a hard slog. Indeed, it may take hardly any work at all if time is on your side. And, once the garden is clear of weeds, there are plenty of labour-saving ways to discourage their regrowth and reduce the amount of regular weeding. These are outlined on pages 20–1. But first, get to know your weeds and the best ways in which to combat them.

KNOW YOUR ENEMY

Weeds divide into two groups: annuals and perennials. Annual weeds grow fresh from seed every year and aren't too much of a problem as they only need killing once. Perennial weeds are the real nightmare because they regrow if even a tiny piece of root is left in the soil. Left unchecked, they run riot and become very hard to get rid of, particularly when they grow through a border of plants. Getting to know which weeds are which may seem difficult at first, but an easy test is to slice off the top of one and see whether or not it grows again. That'll tell you whether you have annual or perennial pests to deal with. Alternatively, ask a gardening neighbour – they're bound to know the major enemies in your area.

Before any planting is done it's hugely important to clear the ground thoroughly, either around mature plants in an established garden or over the entire area of a new one. If you are starting from scratch and aren't in a hurry, the easiest way is to slowly smother your weeds for a year. Otherwise, choose a method of control from the list opposite.

SMOTHER YOUR WEEDS

Getting rid of weeds by the cover-up method requires almost no work – just time and patience – as even the toughest weeds will eventually die if they are deprived of light. All you have to do is mow or cut down the worst of the weeds, then cover the ground with any light-excluding material that is readily available, such as an old carpet, carpet underlay or sheets of cardboard. Heavy-duty black polythene is cheap if bought in bulk. Make sure there's a good overlap at any joins and weigh the edges down or bury them in soil. All light must be kept out.

Cardboard is one of several materials that can be laid on weedy ground to block out light and smother plant growth.

don't allow weeds to seed

Never let weeds grow big enough to seed – one plant can be the parent of hundreds of new ones. The old saying 'one year's seeding is seven year's weeding' holds perfectly true. Although many people think of getting rid of weeds as a summer job, bear in mind that a new generation of annuals will appear in autumn, overwinter as seedlings and mature to set seed by mid-spring.

Rake over the soil before planting to make sure there are no bits of weed root left behind.

After about a year everything underneath the covering should be well dead and it should be fairly easy to dig over the ground. If possible, leave the area bare for a couple of months after digging and before planting. This will give the seeds of annual weeds time to germinate and the seedlings can be hoed off.

CONTROLLING WEEDS

The choice of whether to use weedkillers or not is very much a personal one. Obviously the fewer chemicals that are used in a garden, the better it is for the whole environment, but in some cases they are the only resort. Often the best approach is to use a combination of methods, applying a weedkiller to clean up uncultivated land, and weeding by hand thereafter.

Hoeing Done regularly, this is a wonderfully easy way to control all annual weeds and the seedlings of perennial ones. While the weeds are young, hoe every few weeks during dry weather. Slide the hoe vigorously along the soil's surface to chop off top growth, being careful not to injure nearby garden plants in an established border or tread on newly worked ground.

Digging/hand-weeding Dig out every scrap of the roots of perennial weeds then bin or burn them. In borders, use a trowel or hand fork to dig weeds out from between garden plants.

Contact weedkillers These are only effective against annual weeds as they kill any growth they touch but not the roots. Affects all plants, so take care when applying.

Systemic weedkillers These are used to combat perennial weeds. The chemical is sprayed on to the leaves and the plant then takes the poison right down to its roots. Well-established weeds may need several applications. It is important not to spray garden plants accidentally as they will also be killed, so apply on a windless day and shield nearby plants with wood or cardboard. Perennial weeds growing among garden plants can be treated with a gel form of this type of weedkiller. Either paint it on to the leaves, or put on a pair of tough rubber gloves, smear the gel over the palms and simply pull the stems through your hands. Once again, take care that newly treated weeds don't come into contact with garden plants.

Preventing weeds

The old saying that prevention is better than cure is never truer than when applied to weeds. You can save hours of work by putting down a weed-stopping barrier, such as a mulch.

Listed below is a selection of materials that will keep weeds at bay in beds and borders. Some are fairly costly and very effective, like bark, cocoa shell and membrane, while others are cheap or free but not long-lasting. Before using any of them, make sure the ground is clear of weeds, especially perennial ones, and lay the materials on soil that has had a good soaking. Take care not to pile mulch around plant stems as this can cause rot.

Make your own weed-preventing mulch by shredding woody prunings – remember to stack the shreddings for around six months before use.

MULCHES AND MEMBRANES

Chipped bark An attractive material that makes a really good contrast to border plants. Apply in a layer at least 5cm (2in) thick. Can encourage slugs so preventative measures may be needed, particularly if used around plants like hostas and lilies that attract them.

Cocoa shell Similar in appearance to chipped bark, but is said to repel slugs into the bargain. Apply in the same way as chipped bark.

Garden shreddings You can shred woody prunings to make your own bark mulch. Apply like chipped bark, but stack for 4–6 months before use as freshly shredded material would take plant food from the soil.

Garden compost/well-rotted manure Both these materials suppress weeds when applied in a 10cm (4in) layer and will rot down to improve the soil and help feed plants. However, most garden composts contain some weed seeds.

Mushroom compost Basically horse manure that has been used for growing mushrooms. Often contains lime, so not suitable for use on lime-hating (ericaceous) plants like rhododendrons and azaleas.

Planting membrane Tough, woven plastic sheeting through which holes can be cut for plants, and which lets water through to their roots. Very effective but looks ugly, so disguise it with a thin layer of chipped bark or gravel. Excellent for use on slopes as it helps to stop soil washing away. However, it must be put down before you do any planting and can't be added later!

Black polythene Use as for planting membrane. Cheaper, but it won't let water through, so has to be removed for regular watering.

repel invaders

Sink a permanent barrier into the soil to prevent your garden becoming infested with perennial weeds from outside. Dig a trench at least 30cm (12in) deep next to your fence and line it with a strong material such as stout black polythene or paving slabs, making sure the lining butts up to the base of your fence. Replace the soil, and you'll have a permanent and invisible barrier to repel invaders.

Newspapers/cardboard Lay newspapers or sheets of cardboard around plants. Make sure the edges overlap and keep in place with soil or bark. Lasts for one season only and can then be dug into the ground.

Right: Gravel makes an excellent mulch; lay planting membrane underneath for an effective weed preventer. *Below*: Laid around plants and paving, gravel not only suppresses weeds, but looks attractive too.

Saving water

It's becoming increasingly important to save water. Supply can't meet demand in hot summers and, now that meters are becoming the norm, reducing the amount of water you use is also likely to save you a fair bit of cash.

CHOOSING PLANTS FOR DRY PLACES

Don't even consider planting moisture-loving plants on free-draining soils like sand and chalk that dry out quickly. You'll lock yourself into years of excessive watering and in any event they will never perform at their best on this kind of soil. Put in drought-tolerant plants that really come up smiling when the sun bakes down. (See page 56.) Free-draining soils will hold water more effectively if lots of organic matter is added, and a mulch goes a long way towards reducing the amount of water lost through evaporation.

PLANT IN AUTUMN

Planting in autumn can save lots of watering. Hardy plants like trees, shrubs, perennials, fruits and roses establish best if planted then, when the soil is warm and moist and they can begin to establish a good root system. Come spring, they should only need watering during unseasonably long dry spells. The main exceptions to autumn planting are the less hardy plants, as they really need a whole spring and summer in which to establish before they have to face the winter.

Plants that go in during spring and summer must be kept well watered for months while they put down roots and support fast-growing top growth at the same time.

In a hot garden save on water by choosing plants that suit the situation. Hard landscaping needs no water at all.

where and when to water

During dry weather, use water wisely by concentrating on those plants that will really benefit from it. Prime candidates are any recently planted ones, all plants in containers, thirsty annuals like sweet peas, leafy vegetables and plants that produce fruits. Unless your lawn is the bowling-green type, don't worry about it going brown as it will soon recover (see page 32).

Timing is important, too. Water in the evening or early morning when less water will be lost by evaporation than in the heat of the day – you'll have the added bonus of enjoying a few quiet moments in the garden, too. Give plants a thorough soaking. A sprinkling of water can actually do more harm to plants than none at all because their roots will grow towards the surface in search of what little moisture there is. For younger plants, use a watering can rather than a hose as a powerful jet of water can damage more fragile plants.

WATERING SYSTEMS

Watering systems can be an excellent investment, particularly if you have lots of containers to care for. Try to avoid using a sprinkler as it wastes a lot of water. Instead, use a special perforated hose for borders and a drip system for containers (see page 84).

SAVING AND RECYCLING WATER

Storing rainwater is an excellent way of cutting down on the amount of costly mains water you use. A water butt is the best thing for the job and many inexpensive models are now available. However any large watertight container will do, but make sure it hasn't contained anything nasty that could harm your plants.

Recycled water from baths and washing-up can be used on the garden, but only if it is reasonably clean. It must also be free from detergents, so water from washing machines and dishwashers shouldn't be used.

Set up the water butt next to a drainpipe that is as much out of the way as possible. Where space is really limited you could use a slimline wall-mounted butt.

To set up a standard water butt, stand the butt on a small stack of bricks. They must be high enough to allow you to put a watering can under the tap.

Install a water butt to collect rainwater and cut down the amount of costly mains water that is used.

Use a hacksaw to cut out a section of drainpipe, and connect the butt to the pipe with a rainwater diverter. This diverts water from the drainpipe until the butt is full, then shuts off to let the water go down the pipe to its normal outlet.

Hedges

Tall hedges make wonderful living screens while smaller ones can be lovely structural features within the garden. Although hedges do take time to grow, the bonus is that they increase in beauty over the years as opposed to fences, which are instant in effect but deteriorate as time goes by.

In a windy, exposed position a hedge does a much better job of creating shelter because it filters most of the wind, whereas a solid fence or wall causes it to swirl round on the lee side. If you are planting a hedge in an exposed site you will need a protective barrier of windbreak netting for the first year or two while it becomes established.

A low hedge makes an ideal structural feature. Box (*Buxus sempervirens*) is a popular choice for year-round interest.

plants for formal hedges

PLANT NAME	WHEN TO PRUNE
Buxus sempervirens (box)	Once: early summer
Carpinus betulus (hornbeam)	Once: mid- to late summer
Chamaecyparis lawsoniana (Lawson's cypress)	Twice: spring and autumn
Crataegus monogyna (hawthorn)	Twice: summer and winter
× *Cupressocyparis leylandii* (Leyland cypress)	2–3 times during growing season
Fagus sylvatica (beech)	Once: late summer
Ilex aquifolium (*holly*)	Once: late summer
Ligustrum ovalifolium (privet)	2–3 times during growing season
Prunus laurocerasus (laurel)	Once: spring
Taxus baccata (yew)	Once: late summer

plants for informal hedges

PLANT NAME	WHEN TO PRUNE
Berberis	Immediately after flowering
Elaeagnus	Remove straggly shoots only in spring
Escallonia	Late summer
Lavandula angustifolia	Trim lightly in spring and again after flowering, removing all dead flower stems
Pyracantha coccinea	Summer
Rosa rugosa	Remove thin shoots in spring
Senecio 'Sunshine'	As for *Elaeagnus*
Viburnum tinus	Thin out growth in spring

Many of these plants won't require pruning every year – this is only essential for lavender.

how to trim hedges

1 A hedge that is formally shaped should be kept neat by regular trimming from one to three times a year, depending on the type of plant. Shears are perfectly adequate for trimming small hedges.

2 Larger hedges are best tackled using a hedgetrimmer. Take great care when using any electrically powered tools outside and always use with a powerbreaker device. Keep a particular eye out for children and make sure they're well out of the way before switching on.

3 The fine lines of topiary plants are best trimmed with special pruning shears.

PLANTS FOR HEDGES

The main decision is whether to opt for a neatly trimmed, formal hedge, or one that will be trimmed only to contain growth, or to tidy the overall shape and left to grow informally. Generally, plants for a formal hedge are grown for their attractive foliage, while those for an informal one can be grown for flowers or berries as well as foliage. Bear in mind that while all hedges take up much more space than a fence, an informal hedge takes up more room than a formal one.

Buy and plant hedges in autumn. Not only is this the best time for plants to establish, but many hedging plants are available in bundles at this time and buying them is cheaper than buying individual plants.

PRUNING FORMAL HEDGES

To keep formal hedges to a neat shape, pruning is required once or twice a year – sometimes three times in the case of really vigorous plants like privet or Leyland cypress. Once the plants have grown to the height you require it is vital to start trimming regularly as plants that have been allowed to get out of hand may not regrow if they are pruned very hard.

When trimming a hedge, start at the bottom and work upwards, shaping them so that the bottom is wider than the top. To ensure a really neat finish along the top, rig up a line of string between two upright canes. Leave conifers to grow to about 60cm (2ft) more than the level you want, then cut them back to about 15cm (6in) below that level, so the new growth forms a neat top.

Tools for pruning depend on the size of your hedge as well as your energy levels! Hand shears are usually adequate for small hedges but you may prefer an electric hedge-trimmer for larger jobs. As when working with any electrical equipment outdoors, always use a powerbreaker device and avoid working in wet conditions. Rechargeable models aren't quite so limiting.

Pruning shrubs and roses

Like most things to do with gardening, pruning is rarely as tricky as it appears to be at first glance. Indeed, for several years after making a garden, very little regular pruning will be required but as plants begin to mature and jostle with each other for space, you'll need to take out the secateurs and start to intervene. Some shrubs become horribly woody and bare in the middle when they are old, with all the attractive leaves and flowers stuck on the ends of their branches. Most respond really well to several years of drastic early-spring pruning.

Apart from keeping growth within bounds, pruning should ensure that plants live longer and perform better. Whatever the type of plant, it is important to remove the three Ds – dead, diseased and damaged growth – in order to keep it in good health.

WHEN TO PRUNE

Timing is all – having a pruning blitz at the wrong time of year could mean that you hack off a whole crop of bloom. If you're unsure about when to prune, hold fire until you can establish which plants are which. The major groups of plants needing annual pruning are as follows.

Deciduous shrubs that flower from mid-summer onwards

Cut back hard in early spring to within 5cm (2in) of last year's growth. If you look closely at the shoots you'll be able to see a definite difference between this year's slender smooth-barked shoots and last year's thicker stems with darker, more weathered bark. This group includes buddleja (butterfly bush), hardy fuchsia, lavatera (tree mallow) and sambucus (elder). Shrubs with coloured stems, like *Cornus alba* (dogwood), should be treated in the same way.

Deciduous shrubs that flower from spring to early summer

Prune immediately after flowering has finished, cutting back all the shoots that have borne flowers. This group includes forsythia, *Lavandula* (lavender), philadelphus (mock orange blossom) and weigela.

Evergreen shrubs

These can generally be left to their own devices. Every spring, take a good look at each shrub and cut out any straggly shoots that look at odds with the main body of the plant. Overgrown evergreens should be tackled in mid-spring by removing several large branches as near to the ground as possible. This encourages new growth to come from the base and makes room for the remainder to spread out.

Certain plants need to be pruned every year to stay in shape. Lavender should be trimmed after flowering to avoid its growth becoming straggly and bare at the base.

know your plants

Identifying plants in order to know how to prune them is often the first stumbling block. Buy a pack of labels and a waterproof pen before enticing a gardening friend round to help. Should you be faced with a jungle of unknown plants, it may be worth seeking professional advice.

Overgrown shrubs require drastic pruning, and tools like loppers are great for cutting through branches.

Roses

All roses, except ramblers, should be pruned in early spring. Always remove dead, diseased or damaged growth and cut back weak shoots harder than you would for bush or shrub roses.

Bush roses Cut back shoots to just below knee height.

Shrub roses Remove about a third of the oldest branches, concentrating on those near to the ground.

how to prune a rose

1 Bush roses that are left unpruned quickly become tall and spindly. Pruning should be carried out in early spring.

2 First remove all dead, diseased and damaged shoots. Then, cut all remaining ones back to within 38cm (15in) of the ground.

3 Rambler roses should be pruned after flowering or during winter, cutting out old branches that have borne flowers. If your rambler is not one of the more vigorously growing varieties, you may find you can get away without pruning it at all.

Training climbers and wall shrubs

The one group of plants that really does benefit from attention little and often is those that grow on walls, fences and upright features like pergolas, arches and obelisks. Because most climbers grow upwards by means of twining stems, leaf stalks or tendrils, a plant that is left to its own devices will very soon become a tangled mass. Wall shrubs – shrubs of an upright nature which can be trained on to any vertical support – don't get themselves in a mess as quickly but still need attention several times a year.

CHOOSING A SUPPORT

Most climbers and all wall shrubs need some form of support when growing on walls and fences. The only exception is plants which are self-clinging, although these often need a little help for the first year or two.

Choose between trellis and strong galvanized wire. Trellis comes in a huge selection of styles, sizes and materials and is great for a high-profile spot where you want both the support and the plant to look good. It is also the best choice for small sections of wall. Wire is cheap and long-lasting and by far the best option if you want to cover a large area of wall or fence.

FIXING TRELLIS TO A WALL OR FENCE

If you plan to put trellis straight on to a wall – don't. Use wooden battens to create a gap of at least 2.5–5cm (1–2in) between it and the wall so that plants have room to grow around it. A fence will need occasional access for wood treatment and the trellis should be fixed to it with hinges at the base and hooks at the top. This allows the trellis, complete with plants, to be unhooked and laid down temporarily.

FIXING WIRES TO A WALL OR FENCE

The wires that will support the plants run through rows of vine eyes – screws with a metal loop at one end. Drill holes at intervals of about 1.8m (6ft) in each row, and leave 23–30cm (9–12in) between rows. Use plastic wall plugs on walls, and run the wires close to the lines of mortar so they will barely be seen.

PRUNING CLIMBERS

Many climbers only need pruning when they are overlarge. Thin out the main stems and shorten any that are getting too long. Prune climbers that flower from mid-summer onwards and those with decorative foliage in late winter/early spring. Climbers that flower in spring and early summer are pruned after flowering.

The following plants need pruning every year. Clematis divide into three groups, depending on when they flower.

Trellis makes an ideal support for climbing plants and makes a really attractive feature in its own right.

attatching trellis to a wall

When fixing trellis onto a wall, always use wooden battens or 'spacers' to create a gap of at least 2.5cm (1in) between the wall and the trellis. While the prime reason for this is to allow plant stems to twine freely around the trellis, the improved air movement also helps discourage fungal diseases. Birds really appreciate a bit of plant-protected wall in which to build their nests, too.

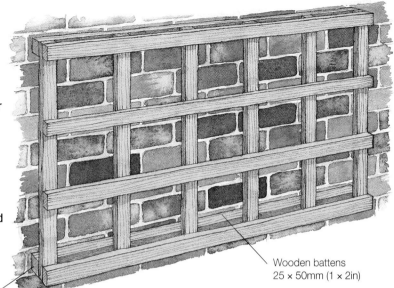

Fixed to wall with screws and wall plugs

Wooden battens 25 × 50mm (1 × 2in)

Clematis group 1 Plants that flower in early summer, and spring-flowering species that flower on growth made the previous year. Prune weak stems by a half to two-thirds in late winter or early spring. Cut overgrown plants hard back at the same time.

Clematis group 2 Plants that flower in mid- to late summer. They can be left unpruned, but cut weak shoots hard back and take the remaining ones back to a strong pair of buds in late winter.

Clematis group 3 Vigorous hybrids and species that flower in late summer. Cut all growth back to about 45cm (18in) off the ground in early spring.

Climbing roses Cut back sideshoots to within 2–3 buds of the main stem. Only prune the main framework branches if they look as though they are outgrowing their site.

Rambler roses Prune immediately after flowering, making sure that you cut out entire branches that have borne flowers.

Wisteria Prune twice a year. In mid-summer shorten sideshoots to around 15cm (6in); in the following mid-winter cut the same shoots back to 2–3 buds.

PRUNING WALL SHRUBS

After flowering, cut back all outward-growing shoots to within two buds or pairs of leaves, and remove shoots that are growing towards the wall. Tie in the remaining stems to the wire or trellis. If the plant has filled its allotted space, prune out the ends of the main stems to fit.

give self-clingers a good start

Climbers like ivy, climbing hydrangeas and Virginia creeper support themselves by means of aerial roots or suckers, but may need a bit of help to get started. After planting, tie the main shoots individually to short bamboo canes. Stand the canes on the ground and spread them out in a fan shape with the tops resting against the wall. Stems that are slow to secure themselves to the wall can be fixed with sticky pads, available from garden centres.

Lawns and lawn equipment

Our garden plants tend to get the lion's share of any tender loving care that's going, but our poor old lawns are all too often abused and ignored, yet still expected to look green and gorgeous. Grass may be functional but it also needs to look good to show off the rest of your garden, in the same way that a well furnished and decorated room needs an attractive carpet rather than a threadbare one. Investing in the right equipment, together with a bit of regular maintenance, will pay dividends and the resulting well-cared-for lawn will set your garden off a treat.

WHAT SORT OF LAWN?

If you're making a new lawn, be sure to choose one that matches your lifestyle. All grasses may look the same but there are different types. Some need lots of care to produce a velvet-like, bowling-green lawn, while others are much harder wearing. Most of us opt for the hard-wearing type that will produce a lawn that can be used and lived on, rather than slaved over. If you have dry soil or a lightly shaded site, you'll need to choose grass to match – this shouldn't be a problem as there are seeds and turf for different kinds of sites. Avoid trying to make a lawn in deep shade. It will never grow well – so opt for shade-tolerant ground-covering plants instead.

WHICH LAWNMOWER?

A lawnmower is the most expensive piece of garden equipment you'll buy, so choose carefully and don't just go for the cheapest one on offer. The main decisions to make are the kind of power you prefer, and the type of cut: do you want a fine, striped lawn or just a neat, plainly mown one? To produce stripes, choose a cylinder mower with a roller. Otherwise, opt for a rotary or hover type. Then decide whether you want a mower with a grass box to collect the clippings. This makes for a better lawn, as otherwise the clippings build up and need raking out every year, and also avoids the irritation of having the clippings trodden indoors.

Mowers come in different sizes, so match yours to the size of your lawn. If it is a large expanse, bear in mind that the wider the cut, the sooner the mowing will be finished – lawnmowers are noisy and you will be thankful if the job gets done quickly. However, the mower must be small enough to cut round corners and flower beds.

OTHER TOOLS FOR LAWNS

Lawn rake A metal springtine rake will do everything you need, from raking out moss and dead grass (known as 'thatch') to clearing up cut grass and leaves.

Half-moon edger For cutting neat, new edges to lawns once or twice a year. A sharp spade can do the job but is much trickier to use.

Always use a half-moon edger on a lawn to create a really neat finish.

mower maintenance

Make sure your lawnmower is in good order before spring or you'll have to wait weeks for a repair during this busy season. If necessary, send it for servicing in winter. Otherwise, check it over, sharpen or replace the blade and oil the moving parts.

Choose a lawnmower with care as it's probably the most expensive piece of garden equipment that you will buy.

Shears For regular trimming of lawn edges. A short-handled pair (see page 10) will be fine if you only have a small lawn. If you have a large lawn, or suffer from back trouble, it is well worth buying a long-handled pair with angled blades. Always clean and dry shears after use.

Strimmer Useful for cutting areas that are difficult or awkward to get to with the mower, such as around the base of garden ornaments and play equipment, under the low branches of trees and on banks. Take care not to strim very close to plants as the nylon line may damage the bark.

type of lawnmower	for	against
Electric	Convenient – plug in and you're off. Many cheap models available. 'Hover' type is the only one suitable for cutting banks.	Nearby electricity source essential. Cable can be restrictive and annoying. Not suitable for large areas as it may overheat. Cheaper models may not last long. Electricity can kill if cable is cut, so do use a powerbreaker device.
Petrol	No restrictions on where it can be used, length of use or area to cover.	Heavier than electric models. Older models can be hard to start.
Push mower	Excellent exercise! Creates no pollution whatsoever and is very long-lasting.	Only practical on small lawns.

Looking after a lawn

Taking care of a lawn is rather like looking after a house – a bit of regular cleaning and then occasional blitzes on certain jobs. With a lawn, the key to success is regular mowing to keep the grass in tiptop condition, along with seasonal jobs like feeding, weeding and leaf-clearing. Some of these are optional, while others, like clearing fallen leaves, are essential.

MOWING DO'S
- Cut grass regularly from spring to autumn. How often depends on the weather – maybe twice a week in a warm, wet spring and once a fortnight during hot, dry spells in summer.
- Mow if necessary in winter but not when the grass is wet or frosty. Brush the lawn first with a broom to scatter wormcasts, set the mower blades high.
- Keep the mower blades sharp.

MOWING DON'TS
- Never mow when the grass is wet.
- Don't scalp your lawn in the hope of stretching the time between mowings. It'll only weaken the grass and let moss and weeds take over.
- Don't cut long grass in one go. Set the blades high and lower them gradually for a second or third cut.

FEEDING THE LAWN
Lawns really benefit from an annual feed, and so will you – strong, healthy grass not only looks green and lovely but also outperforms moss and weeds. Don't starve your lawn in order to reduce the amount of mowing. You may save a couple of days here and there but the resulting poor lawn really won't be worth it.

Feed once in either spring or autumn using a fertilizer designed for that time of year. If you want to do a double whammy of weeding and feeding, there are combination products for this. It is vital to apply fertilizer after a spell of wet weather but when the grass is dry, and to give the lawn a thorough watering if it doesn't rain for a couple of days after this. If you don't, the fertilizer could scorch and kill the grass.

TO WATER OR NOT TO WATER
A 'bowling-green' lawn will need watering during dry spells, but with a hard-wearing type you can leave it to its own devices. If it turns brown, it will green up when wet weather returns. If you do water, do so in the evening or early morning to avoid sun scorch.

'DE-THATCHING' THE LAWN
'De-thatching' (or scarifying) describes the use of a springtine rake to drag out moss and dead grass. Do this a couple of times a year. For larger lawns, it's worth hiring a powered raking machine.

Feed your lawn every year for strong, healthy grass. Use a fertilizer spreader for an even application without waste.

improve lawn drainage

Moss may look green and pleasant but it indicates that your lawn is poorly drained. Applying a moss killer is only a short-term solution – the real answer is to improve drainage. Make lots of little channels in the lawn by sinking a garden fork in to the depth of its prongs and rocking it to enlarge the holes. Repeat the process at 15cm (6in) intervals, then brush sharp sand into the holes to keep them permanently open. It's a lot of work, but should only need doing once.

A well-maintained lawn looks wonderful in a garden of any size.

how to renovate a worn-out lawn

1 Scarify the lawn (see left), then mow and feed with a fertilizer that's suitable for the time of year. Rectify bare patches by seeding them with fresh grass seed. Rake the area first if the surface of the soil is compacted, scatter the seed and cover with a thin layer of compost.

2 Bumps and hollows are a problem when mowing and need to be levelled out. Use a spade to cut underneath the area, then roll back the turf and use a trowel to add or remove soil as necessary.

3 To repair any ragged edges, cut out a piece of turf that includes the damaged area and a good margin of undamaged grass. Using a spade, lift out the turf and turn it round so that the ragged edge is within the lawn. Fill the hole with soil and top with grass seed.

Coping with pests and diseases

While there's no need to get too hung up on the pests, diseases and disorders that may attack your garden plants, it's worth being aware of the common ones that are likely to occur and these are outlined here. If your plants are looking sickly or nibbled, do a bit of detective work to try and establish the cause. Pests are most likely to operate under cover of darkness, so a midnight trip outside with a torch will often reveal the identity of the villains that are chomping away on your plants. Otherwise, take a piece of the affected plant along to the garden centre for advice, or look up one of the many gardening sites on the Internet which feature problem profiles, or even give free advice. A well-illustrated guide to pests and diseases can be useful, but it can also be like a home medical encyclopaedia in that it makes you think you're suffering from a dozen problems rather than one.

PREVENTION RATHER THAN CURE

Plants are like people in that they are more likely to succumb to problems if under stress because of overcrowding, the wrong growing conditions or not enough food or water. That's why emphasis is placed on soil preparation, correct planting, weeding and feeding. Choose the right plants for your garden, plant and care for them properly and you're well on the way to having a garden glowing with health.

Good garden hygiene will also help a lot – try and keep your garden clean and tidy. For example, sweep up dead leaves and fallen flowers where pests can hide, and clean out containers before reusing them as the debris may harbour pests and diseases. If problems do start to become apparent, it's often possible to avoid widespread infection by picking off and binning the bits of plants that are affected. Also bin diseased, fallen fruits as the spores of the disease can overwinter in the soil.

Natural resistance to disease is worth bearing in mind when you buy new plants. Many newer plant varieties have good disease resistance.

METHODS OF CONTROL

Chemical Whether or not to use chemicals to tackle a problem is very much a personal choice. Most persist in the environment to some degree, and the strongest ones may harm nature's own pest controllers, such as birds, frogs, toads and beneficial insects. Where chemicals are the only solution, if possible choose one that targets the problem you are tackling, rather than a broad-spectrum chemical that could kill more desirable insects. Use in moderation and, in the case of a spray, only apply in the evening when few beneficial insects are on the wing.

Biological The use of organisms to tackle specific pests or diseases is now commonplace and has gained in popularity because the method is environmentally friendly. Biological controls are living organisms and have to be supplied fresh, by post. Order either by direct mail or through a garden centre. Follow the instructions carefully to avoid wasting your money.

Physical Many potential problems can be 'nipped in the bud', by keeping an eye on your plants and hand-picking any bits affected. Where relevant, specific measures to tackle certain pests are outlined below.

PESTS

Aphids Often called greenfly or blackfly, these insects appear on young leaves and flowers. They transmit virus diseases between plants and exude a sticky substance – honeydew – that can become covered with black mould. In the early stages, remove clusters of the insects by hand. Treat bad infestations with chemicals.

Slugs and snails These commonplace pests operate at night, munching holes in leaves and consuming whole crops of seedlings. Slug pellets are an effective control but may harm other creatures, even pets. Baits based on aluminium sulphate are more environmentally friendly but less effective. Baited slug traps work reasonably well but need regular attention. There is a biological control that kills only certain types of slugs.

Gathering up slugs and snails by hand on a regular basis can make a difference and is best done on a damp, warm evening. Don't chuck them over the fence – even the slowest snail will make its way back. Certain susceptible plants like hostas and lilies are best grown in containers where they can be protected more easily than if they are growing in the ground.

Vine weevil Until recently, there was no safe and effective chemical to kill this horrendous pest. Plants growing in containers are most at risk. Vine weevil is great at hiding itself away so its presence often goes unnoticed until a plant collapses and dies – the creamy-white grubs live in the soil and munch on roots. The steely-grey adult beetles feed on foliage at night, taking little bites or notches out of leaf edges. The chemical treatment that is now available to kill vine weevil also controls other pests including greenfly and blackfly, and is effective for six months. There is also a biological control.

DISEASES

Mildew There are two types of mildew and they occur in distinctly different conditions:

Powdery mildew This is common on plants that have suffered from drought: they develop a powdery white coating on the upper side of their leaves. Remove the affected parts and spray with a suitable fungicide. Keep the plant well watered – but avoid soaking the foliage – and mulch the ground to improve the soil.

Downy mildew Damp conditions are the root cause of this disease. Downy mildew manifests itself as yellowish areas on the upper side of leaves and corresponding white or purplish coverings underneath. Remove affected parts and spray with a suitable fungicide. Improve the circulation of air by pruning plants to thin out growth.

Viruses These produce a wide range of symptoms including mottled and streaked leaves and distorted growth. There is no cure for viruses; infected plants must be pulled up and binned or burnt.

how to control slugs and snails

1 Pellets are an effective control, but should be used with care, as the poison could affect other creatures. A biological control is a completely safe alternative.

2 Certain plants are more susceptible to attack than others. Hostas are a favourite target; surrounding the plants with sharp grit will provide a degree of protection.

3 Traps baited with beer will kill lots of slugs, but be sure to sink the container into the ground with its rim just above soil level, or you'll also kill ground beetles.

A quick tidy-up

The scene is all too familiar – visitors are expected soon but the garden is a downright mess. You rush outside and stand there flummoxed, not knowing where to start. It's nearly as bad as an unexpected return visit from the *Ground Force* team, but at least you have a bit of warning. However, given a couple of hours to tackle certain areas of the garden you'll soon have a plot that you won't be ashamed of, even if it isn't smart enough to welcome royalty. With a bit more notice and half a day to spare, turn to page 38 to see how to give your garden an instant face-lift.

FIRST THINGS FIRST – THE LAWN
The lawn is central to just about every garden, so one that's neat and tidy will make the world of difference. Cut the grass – in two stages if it has become overlong. Make the first cut with the blades of your

mower set at their highest, pause for as long as possible to let the grass dry, then do the second cut with the blades set lower. Don't try to cut the grass in one go or the lawn will end up a real mess. Cut any remaining long grass that lurks around swings, tree trunks and fences with shears or a strimmer. Finally, trim the edges of the lawn neatly and rake up all the cut grass. If you have a few days' notice, a summer-weary lawn can be perked up a treat with a liquid tonic for grass.

NOW FOR THE BORDER
You will need secateurs and shears, plus stakes and garden string in summer and autumn. Cut off dead flowers – individually with secateurs for large flowers

In gardens where the lawn is a major feature, mowing the grass and trimming the edges makes a world of difference.

like roses, or use shears to trim whole plants such as lavender. Stake and tie plants like tall herbaceous perennials that are flopping badly, and tie in climbers to their supports. Pull up large weeds that look really obvious, but don't get sidetracked by smaller ones unless you have some time to spare. Fill any bare or colourless patches by dropping in a good-looking plant and/or container.

CLEAN HARD SURFACES

A good sweep-up works wonders. Move pots on paving or decking and then replace them, so that you can sweep under as well as around them. Use a hand brush for corners and path edges. Get rid of moss and algae with a special cleaner if time permits, or just give dirty paving a quick going-over with a stiff brush and a powerful jet of water from the hose.

FRESHEN UP GRAVEL

Weedy gravel should really be treated with weedkiller, but for a quick tidy-up pull out the worst of the weeds by hand, loosening the roots with a hoe first to make the job easier, then rake over the gravel to give it a fresh appearance. If you have the time – and a source conveniently close to hand – buy a couple of bags of gravel and spread it around. Be sure to match it with your existing gravel, though.

SET OUT GARDEN FURNITURE

Nothing looks more inviting than garden chairs, table and parasol set out on the lawn – which, of course, should look immaculate by now (you hope). If you only have a couple of faded deckchairs or greying once-white plastic seats, why not treat yourself to new chairs if your budget permits? They needn't be expensive hardwood chairs – canvas ones, for example, are cheap and look extremely good once they are set in place.

Finally, allow a bit of time to smarten yourself up, then take a breather in your freshly tidied garden before welcoming your guests, drink in hand. After all, looking like the *Ground Force* team at the end of two days of hard work would spoil the whole effect.

Sweep all hard surfaces to make the garden look tidy.

INSTANT MAGIC WITH POTS

Containers can make an immediate transformation to any part of the garden and are a great way of ringing the changes with very little work. It pays to stand back and take a fresh look at your containers from time to time, maybe moving and regrouping them so that the plants complement each other. Small pots usually look best in groups, while large ones are often better standing alone where they can be appreciated to the full.

GET RID OF RUBBISH

Gardens have a tendency to become waiting rooms for all sorts of rubbish that builds up over time. Recycle garden waste by composting or shredding where possible; if not, take it to the tip or buy garden waste bags that will be taken by your refuse collector. If there are items, like outgrown children's bikes that are hanging around, sell them or take them to the tip – any useful things will usually be 'recycled' there in any event.

Half-day jobs

Most gardens need a face-lift from time to time, either to repair the effects of wear and tear or to achieve a fresh look. Decide which of the suggestions below are best for you and do some advance shopping so that you have all the necessary materials to hand. None of the jobs should take more than half a day and your garden will undergo a surprising transformation.

HIDE UNSIGHTLY OBJECTS

Every garden contains things that aren't a joy to look at – the dustbin, for example, or buckets that won't fit in the shed. They can be in full view for months, years even, then all of a sudden they have to go!

Give your borders an instant facelift by adding a few large specimen plants, then fill any gaps with seasonal flowers like bulbs and bedding plants.

Instant screens are the answer for eyesores like these. Choose wattle hurdles or brushwood screens for a country-style garden, bamboo or reed ones for modern surroundings. Trellis clothed with climbing plants is another good option, but not an instant one as you'll have to wait while the plants grow.

A drainpipe is trickier to deal with, but there are solutions. Choose from small sections of trellis specially made to go over the pipe; plastic pot-holders that clip on to it; and, if space permits, sausage-shaped growing bags for plants that can be wound around the pipe as they grow.

A manhole is a pain because it must be accessible so that the cover can be removed, even if only once in a blue moon. If it is in soil it can be surrounded by three evergreen trailing plants like junipers or cotoneasters, with long stems that can be pulled aside when necessary. A manhole surrounded by hard surfaces can be hidden under a container of exactly the same size – manufacturers have thoughtfully produced pots to match.

BEAUTIFY YOUR BORDERS

Existing borders often need a bit of 'oomph' to move them up a gear from OK to eye-catching. Sometimes all it takes is a bit of selective plant-replacement: for example, if all the plants are rounded, bring in a bit of drama by removing one or two of them and dropping in a single specimen plant with bold, beautiful foliage, such as phormium (New Zealand flax) or cordyline (cabbage palm). See 'Feature plants', pages 60–1.

Bare patches can be filled with colour at almost any time of year. A visit to the garden centre will turn up lots of seasonal plants like bulbs, annuals, tender perennials and winter bedding-plants. But don't go too mad – a bit of bare ground between plants is no bad thing as it shows off their shapes and colours. Apply a mulch of chipped bark or cocoa shell, and your borders will not only look great but you'll also keep weeds at bay.

liven up a pond

Still water may be tranquil, but moving water is both dramatic and relaxing. If you are one of the many people who are put off fountains by the thought of all that wiring, simply buy a solar-powered pump, sit it in your pond and enjoy! Although it isn't as powerful as an electrically powered model – and costs about four and a half times as much – it involves virtually no work and you may well think this makes it worth the extra expense.

A fountain, or other moving water feature, brings instant life and drama to a still pond and will add interest to your garden even in winter.

how to build a garden feature

1 A tower of attractive stones makes an individual sculpture. Take a length of steel reinforcing rod, about 90cm (36in) long and half-bury it in the ground.

2 Place the drilled stones on the rod so the largest ones are at the bottom, decreasing in size towards the top. Our stones were bought ready-drilled.

3 The final stone is drilled only part of the way through. If you want to fix it securely in place, put some resin in the hole before putting the stone in position.

CONTAINERS

Nothing beats pots for instant gardening and the results can be absolute magic. A selection of permanent plants and seasonal bedding ones, with one plant variety per container, will give the best results year-round. You can simply move the pots to create a fresh look whenever you want one.

INSTANT BULBS FOR BORDERS

Bulbs are unbeatable for spring blooms and will flower for years to come, but there are several drawbacks to planting them directly into borders. First, at planting time in autumn it's not always possible to know where they will look at their best when they bloom in six months' time. Second, once they have flowered you have to put up with weeks of ugly yellowing leaves, as this is how bulbs build up energy for the following year. And, finally, when no growth is visible it's all too easy to spear the bulbs while digging or weeding.

Solve these problems by planting bulbs in containers: either the plastic mesh baskets used for pond plants or planting bags made from plastic membrane. Come flowering time in spring, simply dig holes in bare spots in your borders and drop in both containers and bulbs, making sure the containers are hidden in the soil. Lift after flowering and put in an out-of-the-way spot for the bulbs to die back.

CREATE A CHANGE OF LEVEL

A completely flat garden can be changed dramatically by even a small change of level. The easiest way of doing this is to build a raised bed, either a stand-alone feature, like the one described on page 85, or a larger bed that occupies one corner or a side of the garden.

Strategically placed containers transform any garden. For real drama, splash out on a couple of large, beautifully shaped pots instead of lots of small ones.

Weekend transformations

I f you have an entire weekend to spend in your garden, it's possible to make a huge and long-lasting transformation. Either concentrate on just one major new feature like a pergola, or several smaller projects like putting up a mirror, painting woodwork and making a small water feature. All the following suggestions concentrate on structural aspects of the garden so they will be there for your permanent enjoyment.

CHANGE THE COLOUR OF WOODEN STRUCTURES

These days the great selection of coloured woodstains means there's no need to be confined to boring shades of brown. Features like fences, decking, arches, pergolas – even sheds – can be totally transformed. A word of caution: make sure your chosen colour goes with that of the house and any other buildings, and bear in mind that an unusual one could date very quickly.

BUILD A VERTICAL FEATURE

Upright features like arches, arbours and pergolas make an enormous difference to the look of any garden. Even the smallest, plant-packed space can house one, and there is the added bonus that it creates extra planting space. Lots of these features are available in kit form and are relatively quick and easy to put up, but a bit of advance planning is necessary. Bear in mind that only the smallest kit is likely to fit in a car and so you'll have to allow time for ordering and delivery. And don't forget essential materials like cement and ballast for setting posts. See 'Garden features', pages 118–19.

CHANGE THE SHAPE OF THE LAWN

A lawn is central to almost every garden and its shape dominates the whole plot. Changing this will create a fresh look, with the bonus that there will be more room for plants too.

Many lawns are plain squares or rectangles. Changing the edges to long, gentle curves looks great in informal gardens. It also makes the lawns seem larger. A simple circle or oval looks best and gives lots of planting space around the edges. Conversely, if you want a formal look, squares and rectangles are ideal and look good with a surround such as a path or hedge.

Before actually cutting into the turf, mark out the new shape. Use a rope or hose pipe for curves and string for straight lines. Over the weekend – or longer if possible – look at the shape from every angle, including from upstairs windows, until you're satisfied that it's right.

Transform a boring brown shed with one of the many shades of wood stain designed for outdoor use.

create space with a mirror

Make a small garden seem larger by putting up a mirror. Either set a small one within a piece of *trompe l'oeil* trellis so that it looks like a window on to another piece of garden, or use a full-length mirror to add a feeling of depth. One sited at the end of the path, for example, will make the path appear to continue. A mirror must always be fixed securely, on to a wall or fence, and should be set at a slight angle so that you don't see your reflection as you approach it.

An illusion of space can be created by erecting a mirror so the garden seems to extend into the distance.

make your garden bird-friendly

1 Birds are great fun to watch, and by far the best way to encourage them into your garden is to set up a bird bath or a 'café' in the form of a bird table.

2 A daily supply of food and water will soon become a magnet for all sorts of birds, particularly in winter.

3 Put up several bird boxes around the garden and you may even be lucky enough to have a couple of feathered families setting up home in them.

Doing away with the lawn altogether is another option – and a really practical one if it is so small that it's a pain to mow, or if the grass gets lots of wear. Hard-wearing alternatives include paving, gravel or chipped bark. Herb lawns look and smell wonderful, but will only put up with light use.

MAKE A QUIET RETREAT

A patio is great for sitting out on but sometimes it's just too close to the bustle of the house. All but the tiniest gardens have room for a place in which you can sit, out of sight. Put up two pieces of trellis (a minimum of 1.2m/4ft high) to create an L shape, plant a couple of scented climbers like honeysuckle or jasmine to add to the allure and put a bench in place. Extra refinements could include a couple of slabs to keep your feet dry, and a group of pots on either side of the seat.

Right: An arbour will make a quiet retreat in which to relax.
Below: Your garden can undergo a total change if part or all of the lawn is replaced by another surface.

PLANTS AND PLANTING

The right plant in the right place

There's no doubt that plants are a great investment. They will increase in size and beauty over the years to give your garden that well-established, loved and lived-in look – and time spent on choosing the right ones from the hundreds on offer is never wasted. This chapter shows you how to select the plants that will best suit your garden, and which will thrive with the minimum of work to give colour and interest in every month of the year.

Plants are like people, with different likes and dislikes – in their case, as to where they grow in a garden. A few thrive almost anywhere, but most are to some degree choosy about their sites and the trick is to match their preferences to the conditions in your garden. Follow these basic guidelines before you buy.

Always check out the soil pH – its level of acidity or alkalinity – using a cheap and simple test kit.

- Check out whether the area for planting is in the shade all day or sunny most of the time. Most plants have distinct preferences for one or the other. A site that gets sun for several hours a day is suitable for those that like partial shade.
- Inspect your soil (see below) – if plants like what you can offer them you'll be on to a winner straight away.
- Never be tempted to fight nature and grow plants that aren't suited to your garden, regardless of the fact that it was love at first sight at the garden centre. They're likely to struggle and look sickly for years, involve far too much work and end up being chucked out anyway. You might as well throw your money away in the first place!
- Always remember that, however awkward the conditions in your garden may be, at least a few plants will thrive there.

Most garden centres and nurseries have trained staff who are only too happy to help, so don't be backward about coming forward if you need advice on finding the right plants. The top tip for getting the most attention is to avoid weekends, which are the busiest times, and visit the centre during the week, or on a late night if there is one, when staff are less likely to be rushed off their feet. If weekends are your only free time, try to get to the centre first thing on Saturday.

CHECK OUT YOUR SOIL

Take a fork or spade and dig a few test holes in your garden. If the soil is heavy and sticks together in large lumps it is likely to hold moisture well. Sandy, stony or chalky ground that breaks up easily will dry out quickly. When selecting plants to suit your soil, bear in mind that they need a similar environment right through the year. For example, it's no use growing drought-tolerant plants if the soil is dry in summer but heavy, cold and wet over winter. Similarly, moisture-lovers need ground that is damp throughout the year. All types of soil benefit from a bit of work before planting, and doing this will get your plants off to a flying start in life (see page 15).

A cheap and simple pH kit will determine whether your soil is acid, alkaline or neutral, and to what level, and it is well worth doing this chemical test as certain plants are picky about their soil. The chief culprits are camellias, azaleas, rhododendrons and pieris, all of which hate alkaline or limy soil. However, they can be grown in pots if the soil in your garden isn't suitable for them (see page 94).

Unless stated otherwise, all the plants listed in this chapter do well in any reasonable garden soil.

MIXED BORDERS FOR ALL-YEAR INTEREST

Although summer is the season to get outside and enjoy your garden, when there are masses of eye-catching plants, try to choose plants that also look attractive at other times of the year. Year-round good looks are important for parts of the garden that are seen all the time – like the front garden, for example, or areas that are visible from inside the house.

The best way to create a garden that looks good all year is to plant mixed borders made up of different types of plant: shrubs, conifers, roses, herbaceous perennials, ornamental grasses and bulbs. Not only do they look great throughout the seasons, but they need very little in the way of maintenance. Follow the steps below to create a year-round mixed border:

- Pick out plants that flower at different times, and look for other features like evergreen foliage, colourful or attractively shaped leaves, autumn berries or coloured bark. This way you will be sure to have plenty of colour in every season.
- Choose the largest plants first – they'll be the bones of your border – then fill in the gaps with smaller plants. Any leftover spaces, be they deliberate or accidental, can be packed with seasonal short-lived plants for a splash of colour.
- Check labels for eventual size and place plants accordingly, with tall ones at the back and medium to small ones graduating down to the front.
- Position plants so that their shapes contrast – for example, spiky ones next to rounded and

❀ YOUNG IDEAS

Children are fascinated both by the speed at which sunflowers grow and the huge 'faces' of their flowers. A sponsored sunflower-growing competition is great fun for a pre-school group. The seeds should be sown outside where they are to flower in April or May, although it's also worth sowing a few in pots at the same time in case slugs and snails do their worst. Choose giant varieties that grow in excess of 1.8m (6ft) tall.

The traditional yellow sunflower is still a firm favourite and this easily grown annual is now an ultra-fashionable garden plant.

carpet-forming plants. This means they'll look good whatever the time of year. An easy way to do this is to stand the plants on the ground in their containers and shuffle them around until you're satisfied with the final look.

- Then, and only then, get out your spade and start planting.
- Finally, remember that putting plants together in the best combinations is one of the most challenging aspects of gardening, so take as much time as you need to do this.

PLANTING A GARDEN

Large to medium-sized plants like trees, shrubs and conifers are best planted singly. Smaller ones like perennials, small shrubs, roses and ground-cover plants look far better in groups. Always plant in odd numbers – threes for the bigger plants, fives or sevens for small ones, as this looks far better than lots of lonely singles

dotted about the place. Plant in even numbers only if your garden is a formal design with lots of straight lines.

Placing plants too close to each other is an easy mistake to make, so do space them according to their eventual spread. A border will look almost ridiculously gappy at first, but, once established, the plants will bomb away beautifully. Witness most of the *Ground Force* gardens, where the plants often look few and far between at first but have already filled out a treat when the team returns just a year later. If you want to fill the spaces with flowers, pack in short-lived plants like annuals or biennials. Otherwise, simply cover the ground with a mulch of gravel or chipped bark which will look good and keep weeds at bay.

CONSIDER COLOUR

Talk of colour schemes may seem a bit arty, but all it means is sticking to a handful of colours that you like and which look good together. Less really is more,

how to plant out bedding plants

1 Traditional summer bedding plants, the half-hardy annuals, cannot be planted until after the last frosts have finished. When you're ready to plant them out, water the plants thoroughly while still in their containers to minimize the shock of transplanting. Fork over the ground and rake in a sprinkling of general fertilizer.

2 Tap the sides of the tray and ease out the root-filled wodge of compost. Gently pull the roots apart so that each plant comes away with its own block of soil.

3 Put in the plants, spaced to allow room for growth – generally 23–30cm (9–12in) apart, depending on the type of plant. Water in well. Some protection against slug damage is advisable (see page 34).

because a limited selection of colours is much more effective than a jumble of different ones. Popular combinations that work well include blue, pink, white and cream for a cool and subtle look; blue and yellow for a brighter, yet not overpowering, colour scheme; and vivid shades of red, purple and orange for a hot and almost tropical effect. Look for colourful foliage as well as flowers when you are planning your planting.

How you use colour in your garden can also affect its apparent size. For example, if you want to make a small garden seem bigger, put strong eye-catching colours like red, yellow, purple and orange near the house and pale shades in the distance. Conversely, if the vivid colours are at the end of the garden, the space will look smaller than it actually is.

SCENT, SOUND AND TOUCH

While it's all too easy to become hung-up on what you see in a garden, choose a few plants to please your other senses. Fragrance adds buckets of appeal and comes mostly from scented flowers, but also from aromatic foliage that smells fantastic when it's crushed or bruised. A bit of living, growing aromatherapy will make your garden a wonderfully relaxing place. Gentle background sounds are also relaxing – the splish-splash of moving water, for example, and the swishing sound of leaves and, particularly, grasses and bamboos that rustle in the slightest breeze.

CARING FOR PLANTS

New garden plants must be kept well watered for several months until they've become established, but after that most of them are pretty tough and undemanding. However, all plants benefit from tender loving care. Every year, feed them with a slow-release fertilizer in spring and summer (see page 17), put on a good layer of bulky organic matter in spring (see page 15) and keep down weeds that will compete with them for water and food.

hardiness

Descriptions of plants usually say whether they are hardy or tender. 'Hardy' means a plant should survive the winter outside, while 'frost tender' means it will be killed by frost but can be kept over winter if it's moved under cover. Plants that need a 'sheltered site' must be in a protected spot. If you live in the coldest parts of the country, buy only the hardiest plants. A site near the sea is warmer than an inland one but plants grown there need to be able to tolerate salty winds.

In colder areas, plants like this *Trachycarpus fortunei* palm are unlikely to survive the winter outside. Grow them in containers that can be moved inside for the winter.

Choosing and planting trees

Many gardens have room for only one or two trees and even the smallest of these will be pretty big in comparison to the plants that surround it. If this applies to you, make sure the tree or trees you select earn their keep and look good for a fair part of the year. Don't be tempted by something like a spring-flowering cherry which looks gorgeous for a mere two or three weeks and downright dull for the rest of the year. Choose trees with at least two seasons of interest – spring flowers followed by autumn fruits, for example, or attractive foliage that looks grand from spring to autumn even though it makes less of a show than flowers. For winter, a tree with colourful bark will cheer up the gloomiest days.

Trees come in lots of different sizes and shapes, so spend a bit of time finding one that is right for your garden. Sizes are easy to check out but shapes are often overlooked. While trees that form a rounded head of branches are the most common, there are others that may be better suited to a particular site. For example, an upright variety with upward-pointing branches is perfect if space is limited, while a weeping tree is good where there's room for it to spread widthways but not upwards.

SPRING FLOWERS AND AUTUMN FRUIT

Amelanchier lamarckii Masses of white flowers against bronze-green leaves. The rounded leaves look good throughout summer and develop attractive autumn tints. Black fruits are produced in autumn. Height 5m (15ft).

Malus (crab apple) All flower in spring and produce heavy crops of edible fruit in autumn. The fruit of some varieties often stay on the tree until well into winter. Prefers moist but well-drained soil.

    'Evereste' Red-budded flowers open to white. Heavy crops of red-flushed, orange-yellow fruit that last for a long time. Conical in shape. Height 5m (15ft).

    'Golden Hornet' Pink-budded flowers open to white. Bright golden-yellow fruits remain on the tree for months. Rounded in habit. Height 6m (20ft).

    'John Downie' White flowers and very heavy crops of orange-and-yellow fruits. Upright and broadly columnar in shape. Height 6m (20ft).

    'Van Eseltine' Large flowers are red in bud, opening pink flushed with white. Yellow fruit. Upright and almost columnar in shape. Height 5m (15ft).

Cotoneaster frigidus **'Cornubia'** Clusters of white spring flowers are followed in autumn by heavy crops of red berries. An excellent tree for wildlife – the flowers attract bees, and birds feast on the fruit. One of the few

Amelanchier lamarckii **makes a gorgeous display of spring flowers.**

trees with foliage that is evergreen, unless the winter is severe. Height 4.5m (14ft).

Sorbus All the varieties described below have spring flowers, attractive leaves and autumn berries. Prefers moist but well-drained soil.

S. aucuparia **'Fastigiata'** White flowers and dark red berries. Forms a narrow column of branches. Height 2.4m (8ft).

S. aucuparia **'Sheerwater Seedling'** White flowers and dark red berries. Forms an upright head of branches. Height 6m (20ft).

S. cashmiriana Large clusters of white or pale pink flowers and white, pink-tinged berries. Rounded and slightly spreading shape. Height 5m (15ft).

Trees with attractive foliage like *Pyrus salicifolia* 'Pendula' look good for far longer than those grown for their flowers alone.

S. **'Joseph Rock'** White flowers and yellow-orange berries. Upright in shape. Height 6m (20ft).

TREES WITH ATTRACTIVE FOLIAGE

Acer negundo Varieties like 'Elegans' and 'Flamingo', that have variegated foliage, look lovely from spring to autumn. Summer pruning will encourage a greater proportion of young, colourful foliage. Height 5m (15ft).

Cercis siliquastrum (Judas tree) Rounded green leaves are bronze-purple when young and turn yellow in autumn. Purple-pink flowers are produced too, in late spring. Prefers well-drained soil. Rounded and spreading in shape. Height 5m (15ft).

Gleditsia triacanthos **'Sunburst'** (honey locust) Fern-like leaves appear in late spring, golden-yellow at first, then ageing to light green and becoming yellow again before falling in autumn. Prefers well-drained soil. Broadly conical in shape. Height 10m (33ft).

Malus **'Royalty'** While most crab apples are grown for their flowers or fruit, the main feature of this variety is its deep-purple foliage that turns wine-red in autumn. It also bears crimson flowers in spring and dark-red fruit in autumn. Height 4.5m (14ft).

WEEPING TREES

Malus **'Red Jade'** Flowers are red in bud, opening to white flushed with pink. Small, bright red fruits. A weeping tree that becomes wider than it is high. Height 4m (12ft).

Malus **'Royal Beauty'** Red-purple flowers and dark red fruits. The leaves are reddish-purple when young. Weeping and compact in shape. Height 2.4m (8ft).

Prunus × *yedoensis* **'Shidare-yoshino'** (Yoshino cherry) Masses of blush-pink, delicately scented flowers cover the branches in early to mid-spring. This tree has a particularly graceful shape with arching branches falling in curtains to the ground. Spread 2.4m (8ft).

Pyrus salicifolia **'Pendula'** (weeping pear) Silvery leaves from spring to autumn, plus white spring flowers. Prefers moist, well-drained soil. Forms a rounded head of branches that weep to the ground. Height 5m (16ft).

Salix caprea **'Pendula'** (Kilmarnock willow) A wonderful sight in early spring when the branches are smothered in silvery, silky catkins that eventually turn yellow with pollen later in spring. Height 1.8m (6ft).

Salix purpurea **'Pendula'** (weeping purple willow). A small, neat tree with slender reddish-purple branches that are covered in small catkins in early spring, which are followed by slender, pointed leaves. Both these willows are compact varieties that grow to around 1.8m (6ft), unlike the much, much larger weeping willow (*Salix* × *chrysocoma*).

trees with attractive bark

Eucalyptus pauciflora subsp. *niphophila* (snow gum) develops beautiful patterns on its trunk as the tree matures. This quick-growing tree is one of the hardiest of the many different *Eucalyptus* species. Height 6m (20ft).

Acer griseum (paper-bark maple) is a supremely attractive tree with its peeling, cinnamon-coloured bark. However, this is a tree for the patient gardener as it will take a good few years to reach a decent size. Height 3m (10ft).

Betula utilis var. *jacquemontii* (Himalayan birch) Most dazzling of the birches with gleaming white bark. Widely conical in shape. Height 10m (33ft). To see this tree at its best, site where the winter sun will shine upon its trunk.

PLANTING A TREE

Trees establish best when planted in autumn or during mild spells in winter. At this time it's possible to buy bare-rooted or rootballed trees that have been grown in a nursery field and lifted while they are dormant. Such trees offer good value for money, particularly if you want to buy a large specimen.

Container-grown trees are available all year and can be planted at any time, but it is vital that they are kept well watered if planted whilst in active growth. Most trees in containers are designed to be easily transportable, consequently they are relatively small and compact in size. Look around for the most reasonably priced, healthiest trees before you buy.

Trees that are planted during spring and summer, while in full growth, must be kept well watered during any dry spells.

planting a tree

1 Soak the rootball before planting. Put the tree in the planting hole which has been dug larger than the rootball, and make sure the tree is planted at the same level as it was growing previously.

2 A tree needs staking during its early years while it puts down roots. Knock in a short stake at an angle to the trunk, taking care not to spear the rootball.

3 Secure the stake to the tree using a wide plastic tree tie. Check the tie every so often in case of rubbing, particularly with a tall tree like this one.

Shrubs for flowers and foliage

Shrubs form the skeleton of a planting scheme and are the hardest working plants in the garden. With a few exceptions, they last for many years and need next to no looking after. Look for shrubs with flowers or attractive deciduous or evergreen foliage to be sure of a selection that will see you right through the year.

FLOWERING SHRUBS

Some of the shrubs listed below have evergreen leaves, but flowers are their main feature. Choose shrubs that bloom at different times of year so that you get a succession of colour. With the exception of the evergreens, they all lose their leaves in autumn.

Spring/early summer flowers

Daphne odora **'Aureomarginata'** Clusters of small pink-and-white flowers with a strong lily-of-the-valley scent are borne for many weeks. Handsome all year with evergreen, cream-edged leaves. Full sun. Height 1m (3ft).

Hebes come in many sizes. This variety, 'Margret' is neat, compact, and flowers for months.

Exochorda × *macrantha* **'The Bride'** Masses of pure white flowers borne in large clusters along arching branches. Sun/part shade. Height 1.5m (5ft).

Philadelphus There are many varieties of the popular mock orange blossom, which bear masses of strongly scented white flowers. 'Manteau d'Hermine' only grows to 1m (3ft) while others like 'Virginal' reach in excess of 2.4m (8ft). Sun/part shade.

Prunus incisa **'Kojo-no-mai'** The name translates as 'flight of butterflies' – you can see why when the upright, zigzag branches are wreathed in pale pink flowers. The leaves develop lovely autumn tints too. Sun/part shade. Height 1m (3ft).

Rhododendron yakushimanum **hybrids**
A group of small yet handsome rhododendrons with bold, handsome leaves and clusters of large flowers in a variety of attractive colours. Evergreen. Needs an acid, moist but well-drained soil in part shade. Height 1m (3ft).

Syringa Lilacs make a lovely spring display of scented flowers but many varieties become very large. Good small lilacs are *S. meyeri* var. *spontanea* 'Palibin' (lavender-pink), height 1.2m (4ft), and *S. pubescens* subsp. *microphylla* 'Superba' (pink), height 1.8m (6ft). Sun.

Viburnum The 'snowball' varieties are spectacular, as well as scented, bearing huge heads of white or pink-tinged flowers. Species to look for are *V.* × *burkwoodii*, *V. carlesii*, *V. carlcephalum* and *V.* × *juddii*. Height 1.2–2.4m (4–8ft).

Summer/autumn flowers

Buddleja davidii (butterfly bush) Fast-growing shrub that bears long cone-shaped flowers in colours that include white, pink, purple and blue. Butterflies flock to its nectar-rich blooms, hence its name. Sun and well-drained soil. Height 2.4m (8ft).

Caryopteris × *clandonensis* **'Heavenly Blue'** Upright plant bearing masses of spiky, deep blue flowers that

dry-weather planting

Keep plants that go in during spring and summer watered during dry spells, right through to autumn. If you have to plant when the ground is dry, first soak the soil by emptying a couple of buckets of water into the planting hole and letting it drain away before the plant goes in.

Before you backfill with soil, take a large plastic bottle, unscrew its top and cut off its base. Put it upside down in the hole next to the plant and fill round it with soil so that only a bit of the bottle is visible. Fill the bottle at every watering to ensure that the water goes straight down to the roots.

When putting in plants like this *Tamarix* 'Pink Cascade', it's vital that the plant never grows short of water until the roots are established.

show off well against grey-green leaves. 'Worcester Gold' has the added bonus of golden leaves. Prefers light, well-drained soil, and sun. Height 1m (3ft).

Ceratostigma willmottianum Low, spreading plant that bears brilliant blue flowers which last into autumn, when the leaves turn deep red. Prefers sun and light soil. Height 45cm (18in).

Cytisus (broom) Fast-growing but fairly short-lived shrub with flowers in many bright colours, either single shades or bicolours. *Cytisus × praecox* (Warminster broom) bears its yellow flowers in early summer, while other hybrids bloom in mid-summer. Needs sun and well-drained soil. Height 1.2–1.8m (4–6ft).

Escallonia 'Iveyi' Most handsome of all the escallonias, with large clusters of white flowers against glossy, evergreen foliage. Sun. Height 2.4m (8ft).

Fuchsia (hardy varieties) Not to be confused with frost-tender varieties of fuchsias. There are many hardy ones that stay outside all year, though they do prefer a sheltered spot in full sun. Masses of colourful blooms dangle underneath gently arching stems. Height 60–90cm (24–36in).

Hebe There are lots of different varieties of this long-flowering evergreen shrub, ranging in size from 30cm (12in) to 1.5m (5ft), with flowers of white, pink, blue and purple. Larger varieties do best in a sheltered site. Sun.

Lavandula Popular for its fragrant flowers and aromatic leaves, lavender comes in white and pink varieties but blue is most people's favourite. Watch out for *L. stoechas* (French lavender) as it's more tender than most and needs a sheltered site. Grow in sun and well-drained soil. Height 45–60cm (18–24in).

drought-tolerant plants for light, free-draining soils

Plants have adapted to deal with drought in a variety of ways. Silver-leaved plants mostly have woolly or hairy leaves to reduce water loss, like *Artemisia ludoviciana* 'Silver Queen'.

Woolly stems topped with rounded blue flowers make *Echinops bannaticus* (globe thistle) a dramatic plant for a dry spot.

Thick, fleshy leaves enable plants like *Sedum* 'Herbstfreude' to store water for times of drought.

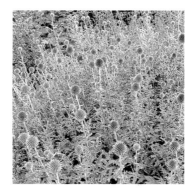

Lavatera The 'tree mallows' are exceptionally long-flowering and quick-growing, but only tend to last for a few years. Good varieties include 'Barnsley' (pale pink, darker centre), 'Blushing Bride' (pale pink with grey leaves), 'Burgundy Wine' (dark pink) and 'Ice Cool' (white). Grow in sun and well-drained soil. Height 1.8m (6ft).

Potentilla fruticosa Long-flowering shrub bearing masses of saucer-shaped flowers right through summer and into autumn. Some varieties are low-growing and spreading, suitable for the front of the border, while taller ones are good mid-border plants. Colours include white, yellow, pink, orange and red. Grow in sun. Height 60cm–1.2m (2–4ft).

Winter flowers

Lonicera × *purpusii* **'Winter Beauty'** This shrubby honeysuckle is nothing much to look at for most of the year, but come winter it is smothered with creamy-white tassels of scented flowers. Sun/part shade. Height 1.5m (5ft).

Mahonia Spiny-leaved evergreens with large, handsome leaves, bearing bright yellow, sweetly scented flowers through late winter and into early spring. Smaller varieties include *M. aquifolium* 'Apollo' and 'Smaragd', while larger ones include 'Charity' and 'Lionel Fortescue'. Sun or shade. Height 1–1.8m (3–6ft).

Sarcococca Masses of tiny, deliciously scented, creamy-white flowers are borne in mid- to late winter. A neat and tidy little evergreen that looks good all year. Happy in sun or shade. Height 60cm (24in).

Skimmia japonica **'Rubella'** Dome-shaped evergreen with red-tinged leaves. Attractive dark red flower buds produced in autumn look good for months and eventually open to creamy-white flowers in late winter. Part or full shade. Height 1m (3ft).

Viburnum tinus **'Eve Price'** (laurustinus) Large heads of creamy-white, pink-budded flowers open in mid- to late winter and last for months. Glossy evergreen leaves look good all year. Grow in sun or part shade. Height 1.8m (6ft).

SHRUBS WITH DECIDUOUS FOLIAGE

Deciduous shrubs with coloured or attractively shaped foliage are great for new gardens as they grow faster than evergreens. Their leaves look good from spring to autumn and, as well as being attractive in their own right, they make an excellent backdrop to flowering plants.

Artemisia **'Powis Castle'** Forms a low mound of lacy, silver foliage which is aromatic when crushed. Needs well-drained soil and full sun. Height 60cm (24in).

Berberis thunbergii Prickly shrubs with small leaves in green, pink, purple or gold. Different varieties vary in size. Smallest is 'Atropurpurea Nana' (purple leaves), then comes 'Bonanza Gold' (golden yellow), 'Dart's Red Lady' (purple), 'Rose Glow' (pink and white) and 'Silver Beauty' (green and white). Largest of all is 'Atropurpurea' (red-purple). Sun or part shade. Height 60cm–2.4m (2–8ft).

Cornus alba (dogwood) An all-year shrub with attractive red stems that look good all winter and coloured leaves for spring to autumn interest. 'Aurea' has golden foliage, 'Elegantissima' is green and white, 'Spaethii' is yellow and green. Sun or part shade. Height 1.8m (6ft).

Cotinus (smoke bush) A large shrub with rounded leaves that look good through spring and summer, peaking in autumn by turning spectacular shades before falling. Mature plants produce large clusters of tiny flowers in late summer that look like puffs of smoke. Varieties include 'Golden Spirit' (bright golden-yellow leaves, orange and red autumn colour), 'Grace' (soft purple turning scarlet in autumn), 'Royal Purple' and 'Velvet Cloak' (deep purple, turning bright red in autumn). Grow in sun or part shade. Height to 3m (10ft).

Physocarpus opulifolius Rounded shrub with lobed leaves in gold or purple. 'Diablo' is deep purple, 'Dart's Gold' is bright yellow when young, ageing to yellow-green. Sun or part shade. Height 1.5m (5ft).

Sambucus (ornamental elder) Two varieties look very decorative. *S. nigra* 'Black Beauty' produces purple leaves, plus heads of pink flowers in summer. *Sambucus racemosa* 'Plumosa Aurea' has finely cut leaves that open bronze-yellow and age to gold, plus white summer flowers. Sun or part shade. Height 2.4m (8ft).

Santolina pinnata* subsp. *neapolitana (cotton lavender) Rounded shrub with finely divided silver leaves, plus yellow, button-like flowers in summer. Needs sun and well-drained soil. Height 60cm (24in).

Spiraea japonica Rounded shrubs with bright foliage and pink flowers in summer. Good varieties are 'Candle Light', 'Fire Light', 'Golden Princess' and 'Goldflame'. Sun. Height to 75cm (30in).

PLANTING A SHRUB

The ideal time to put in most shrubs is autumn. The exceptions are evergreens that need a sheltered site, which should be planted in spring.

Before planting, soak the roots by standing the plant in a bucket of water for an hour or so. Dig a planting hole slightly larger than the rootball and mix some planting compost into the hole and into the excavated soil. Take the plant out of its pot. If there are lots of roots spiralling around the bottom of the rootball, gently tease them loose.

Put the plant in the hole so that the top of the rootball is level with the ground, backfill around the roots with the soil and firm it gently with your heel. Water well.

Add planting compost to the hole and the excavated soil for backfilling. This encourages roots to grow outwards from a rootball, which contains fine potting compost, into the harsher environment of garden soil.

Evergreen shrubs and conifers

Plants with leaves that look attractive all year round are the true bones of a garden. Not only are they eye-catching during winter, but from spring to autumn they form a backdrop for flowering plants. About a third of your larger plants should be evergreens; any more and your garden could look as though it never changes. Low-growing evergreens for ground cover are on page 75.

EVERGREEN SHRUBS

Aucuba japonica (spotted laurel) Tough shrub with large, glossy leaves in a variety of colours. Brightest of all is 'Crotonifolia' with gold-splashed leaves, while 'Rozannie' has glossy green leaves and red berries. Grow in part shade. Height 1.5m (5ft).

Evergreens of all sizes are a vital part of the garden's structure. *Buxus sempervirens* (box) is excellent whether grown individually or as a low hedge.

Buxus sempervirens (box) Versatile, small-leaved evergreen that's great for trimming into all sorts of shapes (see 'Topiary', page 61), and makes a good low hedge. Varieties with gold or white colouring include 'Aureovariegata', 'Argenteovariegata' and 'Elegantissima'. Sun or part shade. Height to 1.2m (4ft).

Choisya ternata (Mexican orange blossom) Popular for its fragrant white flowers, the glossy, lobed leaves look wonderful all year. 'Aztec Pearl' has the best leaf shape and is the smallest, 'Sundance' has bright yellow leaves. Grow in sun and in a sheltered site. Height 1.2m (4ft).

Elaeagnus Rounded or upright shrubs with large, leathery, silver or golden-variegated leaves. *Elaeagnus* × *ebbingei* has metallic green leaves, 'Gilt Edge' and *E. pungens* 'Maculata' are green and gold. Grow in sun or part shade. Height 1.8m (6ft).

***Lonicera nitida* 'Baggesen's Gold'** Bushy shrub with arching branches, covered in tiny, bright yellow leaves. Can be trimmed to a neat dome if preferred. Also makes a good low hedge. Grow in sun or shade, but avoid wet soil. Height 1.5m (5ft).

***Ligustrum ovalifolium* 'Aureum'** (golden privet) While green privet should be avoided like the plague, golden privet is often unfairly ignored. Vigorous, tough and easy to grow, this green-and-gold shrub can be trimmed to shape, grown as a hedge or just left to form a large, graceful bush. Sun or shade. Height to 2.4m (8ft).

***Photinia* × *fraseri* 'Red Robin'** Large, upright shrub with glossy green leaves and showy, bright red young shoots. Sun or part shade. Height 3m (10ft).

***Rhamnus alaternus* 'Argenteovariegata'** Large, conical shrub with small grey-green leaves that are edged with white. Can be trimmed to shape if desired. Grow in sun and well-drained soil. Height 2.4m (8ft).

Viburnum davidii Mound-forming shrub with large, dark green leaves that are attractively ridged. Some plants bear turquoise berries in autumn. Sun or part shade. Height 1m (3ft).

Yucca Handsome, architectural plant that forms a clump of sword-like, fleshy leaves. The tips are very sharp so watch your eyes when weeding! There are green-leaved varieties but coloured ones like 'Bright Edge' and 'Golden Sword' look best. Huge creamy-white flowers may be produced in a hot summer. Grow in a sheltered, sunny site, on well-drained soil. Height 75cm (30in).

CONIFERS

Conifers come in all manner of shapes, sizes and colours and make fantastic structure plants. They were all the rage back in the 1970s when whole borders were given over to them but, like most things that reach the height of fashion, they've been largely ignored ever since – rather like flares and kipper ties. Nowadays most people prefer to scatter a few of them through a border with other types of plants. Conifers are especially good alongside herbaceous perennials and ornamental grasses: in summer their solid outlines and colours make a lovely background to the airy flowers and foliage of the perennials and grasses – which die back in winter to reveal the full beauty of the conifers.

Conifers vary enormously in size, from tiny little dwarfs suitable for rock gardens to massive specimens that will top 15m (50ft). Trouble is, they look very similar when young so it's important to read the label carefully and make sure you're not buying a baby giant. Their shapes also vary, from carpeting and spreading plants to pillars, pyramids and cones. Foliage colours are mostly greens, golds and blues, though a few varieties change colour from summer to winter.

WHEN TO PLANT EVERGREENS

The best time to plant hardy evergreens is early to mid-autumn. Those that are described as needing a sheltered site should be planted in spring. Plants going into a windy, exposed site should be protected with a screen of windbreak netting for the first year or two, as cold winds can dry out and scorch their foliage. This netting is readily available from garden centres and mail-order suppliers. See page 57 for planting details.

Spiky leaved evergreens like *Yucca gloriosa* make magnificent specimens for containers and thrive in a hot, sunny site. Beware the leaf tips, which can be very sharp.

conifers for shape and colour

- *Chamaecyparis lawsoniana* 'Gimbornii' Rounded, grey-green, dwarf
- *C. obtusa* 'Pygmaea' Rounded, bright green, small
- *C. thyoides* 'Ericoides' Conical, green with purple winter tints, small
- *Juniperus communis* 'Sentinel' Narrow and upright, blue-green, small
- *J.* × *pfitzeriana* 'Gold Sovereign' Spreading, golden-yellow, small
- *J. scopulorum* 'Skyrocket' Slender, grey-green, tall
- *J.* × *squamata* 'Blue Carpet' Spreading, silver-blue, medium
- *Picea glauca* 'Alberta Blue' Conical, silver-blue, small
- *Taxus baccata* 'Standishii' Columnar, golden-yellow, small
- *Thuja plicata* 'Atrovirens' Conical, dark green, tall

Feature plants

Almost all *Ground Force* gardens include a few large, well-grown specimen plants with bold, spiky leaves or handsome architectural shapes, to create an immediate impact and give a newly made-over garden a feeling of maturity. Of course, ready-grown specimens like these usually cost a packet as a plant nursery will have spent years growing them. However, if you're not in a hurry for an instant effect you can start with smaller, cheaper plants and grow them on to become features in your garden.

All the plants described here can be grown either in the ground or in large containers. Certain plants can't be left outside all year in cold areas and are best grown in pots and moved into an unheated porch, greenhouse or conservatory for the winter.

A tree fern makes a magnificent specimen plant that adds a touch of real drama to a shady site.

Cordyline australis (cabbage palm) Not a true palm tree, but it resembles one in that it forms a head of spiky evergreen leaves and develops a clear trunk as it grows. Varieties with attractively coloured leaves include 'Albertii' (striped green, red, cream and pink), 'Purple Tower' (plum-purple) and 'Torbay Dazzler' (green striped with cream). Needs to go under cover for winter in cold areas. Grow in full sun. Height to 3m (10ft).

Dicksonia antarctica (tree fern) This spectacular plant isn't cheap but does transform a garden, with its brown, fibrous trunk topped with long, leafy fronds. Grow outdoors all year only in mild areas or sheltered sites, otherwise grow in a container and bring under cover for winter. Needs acid soil rich in organic matter, in partial or full shade. During hot weather, hose the trunk (but not the leaves) with water, daily. Height to around 1.8m (6ft).

Feature plants are packed with personality and will give any part of the garden a real lift. *Cordyline australis* (cabbage palm) brings an exotic touch to the border.

Ilex (holly) Many hollies have attractively shaped leaves and make wonderful specimen shrubs. They can be kept small, and trimmed to different shapes, or left to develop into small trees. Only female varieties bear berries, and you'll need a male as well to be sure of a good crop. Sun or part shade. Height 3.6m (12ft).

Miscanthus sinensis This tall ornamental grass has slender, upright clumps of stems. It dies back to the ground in autumn and regrows in spring. The leaves are sometimes striped or variegated, as with 'Gracillimus' and 'Morning Light', or banded as in the case of 'Zebrinus'. Decorative heads of 'flowers' are borne in late summer. Grow in sun. Height 1.2m (4ft).

Phormium (New Zealand flax) Forms large, upright clumps of long, slender leaves. Choose from different leaf colours, like 'Cream Delight' (green striped with cream), 'Dazzler' (bronze striped with red, orange and pink), 'Sundowner' (bronze-green edged with pink) and 'Yellow Wave' (yellow-green). Grow in full sun and bring under cover for winter in cold areas. Height 1–1.8m (3–6ft).

BAMBOOS

Tall bamboos forming clumps of slender canes clothed with delicately shaped foliage. They look striking, make excellent screening or specimen plants – and the leaves rustle soporifically in the slightest breeze.

Fargesia murieliae (umbrella bamboo) Bright green leaves and yellow-green stems that arch with age. Grow in sun or part shade. Height to 3m (10ft).

F. nitida (fountain bamboo) Dark green leaves and dark, purple-green canes. Prefers partial shade and shelter from cold winds. Can spread rapidly. Grow in a container if this could be problematic. Height to 4.2m (15ft).

Phyllostachys aurea (golden bamboo) Golden-green leaves and canes that are bright green when young, then turn yellow-brown. *P. nigra* (black bamboo) has dark green leaves and green canes that age to a striking shiny black colour. Grow in sun or light shade, sheltered from winds. Height to 3m (10ft).

Ready grown specimen plants, like this bamboo, don't come cheap, but it can be worth splashing out on a couple of plants that will give an air of maturity to a new garden.

TOPIARY

Topiary is a fancy name for clipping or training plants into different shapes. Topiary plants look fantastic all year and really add style to any garden, whether they are grown in the ground or in containers.

Ready-grown topiary is widely available, but at a price. Growing your own isn't difficult, but it takes several years to get a plant into shape by trimming it in spring, early summer and maybe also late summer. The best plant for all sorts of shapes is *Buxus sempervirens* (box). For simple shapes there's a wide choice that includes *Laurus nobilis* (bay), *Viburnum tinus* (laurustinus) and *Ligustrum ovalifolium* 'Aureum' (golden privet).

Take a short cut to style by using a wire topiary frame. These come in all sorts of shapes and are available from garden centres. Train two or three decent-sized ivies around the frame and, within just a year or two, you'll have a topiary plant that will be a real talking-point. See page 57 for planting details.

Climbers and wall shrubs

Climbing plants are enormously versatile and can be grown in lots of different places. Apart from obvious sites such as walls and fences, climbers on features like arches, arbours and pergolas create a whole new dimension in a garden and give it a stunning new look. On a smaller scale, freestanding supports such as obelisks and wigwams can be easily dropped into borders for instant height. Even well-established trees, shrubs and conifers can be given an extra garland of flowers if you grow climbers through their branches.

On a practical note, climbing plants can be used to make beautiful living screens, ideal for creating privacy and perfect for hiding anything you'd really rather not look at – like the dustbin. And they are fantastic plants for small gardens because they produce loads of growth yet only occupy a tiny area of ground. Compact varieties can even be grown in containers (see page 95). Wall shrubs – plants that benefit from the support of a wall or fence – can be trained upwards on wires or trellis. Regular tying-in of growth and pruning of outward-facing shoots will keep them close to their support. These shrubs are often sold alongside climbers in nurseries and garden centres.

All climbers and wall shrubs, bar a few self-clinging varieties, need some form of support such as trellis or galvanized wire run-through vine eyes (see page 28). And remember that many of them have distinct preferences for sun or shade, so be sure to match the right plant to the right place.

See also clematis (pages 66–7) and roses for vertical structures (page 69).

scented flowers

Fragrance should never be overlooked when planning a garden. The flowers of some plants don't have to be showy to smell good; your nose will find the blooms of *Elaeagnus* × *ebbingei* 'Limelight' long before your eyes do.

Some scented beauties are small-scale charmers and benefit from being grown in a rock garden or raised bed, like *Daphne cneorum* 'Eximia'.

Climbing plants with fragrant flowers like *Lonicera japonica* 'Halliana' can be trained on arbours and pergolas to give a waft of perfume to anyone sitting beneath.

YOUNG IDEAS

Fast-growing and colourful climbers are the ideal first-time plants for child gardeners. Two easy hardy annuals to raise from seed are sweet peas (*Lathyrus odoratus*) and nasturtiums (*Tropaeolum majus*). The sweet peas can be sown in pots in autumn or late winter/early spring, and both plants can be sown directly outside in early spring. They must be grown in a sunny site and can be trained up some form of support, like trellis or a 'wigwam' of bamboo canes. Nasturtiums prefer poor soil and only need watering in very dry seasons, while sweet peas like rich soil plus regular watering and feeding.

CLIMBING PLANTS FOR FULL SUN

Many exotic-looking plants need a south-facing site in order to do well. In cold areas they should only be grown against a wall where the 'storage-heater' effect of the bricks will give protection from the cold in winter.

Ceanothus (Californian lilac) Bushy wall shrub that makes a spectacular show of flowers in early or late summer, depending on the variety. Needs well-drained soil. Height 2.4m (8ft).

Clematis cirrhosa In complete contrast to the majority of clematis, this species is evergreen and blooms in late winter to early spring, bearing small, cup-shaped flowers that nestle among the lobed leaves. White, cream and red-splashed varieties are available. Height 2.4m (8ft).

***Fremontodendron* 'California Glory'** Wall shrub that makes a glorious display of large, bright yellow, waxy petalled flowers in early to mid-summer. Needs well-drained soil. Evergreen. Height 3.6m (12ft).

Ipomoea tricolor (morning glory) Colourful frost-tender annual that bears large saucer-shaped flowers through summer. 'Heavenly Blue' is the most popular variety, with beautiful sky-blue flowers. Height 1.8m (6ft).

Passiflora caerulea (passion flower) Vigorous climber with spectacular and unusually shaped blue-and-white flowers that show up well against handsome, dark green lobed leaves. 'Constance Elliott' has ivory white flowers. Orange fruits are borne after a hot summer. Evergreen/semi-evergreen. Height 5m (16ft).

***Solanum jasminioides* 'Album'** (potato vine) Twining climber that bears clusters of pure white flowers with golden stamens, from mid-summer to autumn. Deciduous. Height 4m (13ft).

Teucrium fruticans (shrubby germander) Wall shrub that bears many mid-blue flowers in summer that contrast well with small silvery-grey leaves. Needs well-drained soil. Evergreen. Height 1.8m (6ft).

Trachelospermum asiaticum Self-clinging climber that flowers through summer and often into autumn, bearing creamy-yellow, jasmine-like flowers that have a delicious scent. Glossy evergreen foliage. Height 2.4m (8ft).

Wisteria floribunda Twining climber that makes a superb show of large, dangling racemes of scented violet-blue flowers in early summer. Attractive divided foliage. Deciduous. Height 5m (16ft).

Hedera Helix 'Buttercup' is one of the most attractive golden ivies.

CLIMBING PLANTS FOR SUN/SHADE

East- and west-facing sites receive sun for part of the day and are suitable for a range of plants, including all those listed in the next section with the exception of the hydrangea and honeysuckle. West-facing sites are warmer than east-facing ones and in mild areas they are also ideal for the plants for full sun described on page 63.

Humulus lupulus **'Aureus'** (golden hop) Vigorous twining climber with large lobed leaves that are golden-yellow in spring, ageing to lime yellow. Dies back to ground level in winter and regrows in spring. Height 4m (13ft).

Jasminum officinale (summer jasmine) Vigorous climber bearing clusters of pure white, scented flowers through summer. 'Fiona Sunrise' also has attractive golden foliage. Deciduous. Height 3–4m (10–13ft).

Lonicera (honeysuckle) There are many varieties of this gorgeously scented summer-flowering climber. It prefers to have its roots in the shade and its 'head' in the sun. Deciduous. Height 4m (13ft).

Parthenocissus (Virginia creeper) Vigorous self-clinging climber with attractive lobed or divided leaves that turn fiery shades of orange and red in autumn. Deciduous. Height 6m (20ft).

Pyracantha (firethorn) Thorny wall shrub that bears clusters of white flowers in spring followed by yellow, orange or red berries, depending on variety. 'Saphyr' varieties are resistant to the scab disease that troubles some older varieties. Evergreen. Height 3.6m (12ft).

Tropaeolum peregrinum (Canary creeper) Easy and fast-growing hardy annual climber that produces numerous bright yellow flowers through summer. Height 2.4m (8ft).

Vitis coignetiae (ornamental vine) Vigorous climber with enormous and attractive dark green leaves that develop orange and red autumn colours. Deciduous. Height 7m (23ft).

CLIMBING PLANTS FOR SHADE

A shady, north-facing site is often perceived as being difficult but plenty of attractive plants thrive out of the sun. There is also the bonus that flowers last longer out of direct sunlight.

Chaenomeles (flowering quince) Attractive wall shrub that bears numerous clusters of small, saucer-shaped flowers along its thorny branches in spring, before the leaves appear. Large fruits are produced in autumn and can be used in preserves. Flower colours include red, orange, pink and white. Deciduous. Height 1.8m (6ft).

Hedera colchica (Persian ivy) Vigorous self-clinging climber with large, glossy lobed leaves. Variegated varieties look most attractive: 'Dentata Variegata' is green and white while 'Sulphur Heart' (also known as 'Paddy's Pride') has a bold central splash of lime yellow. Evergreen. Height 5m (16ft).

Hedera helix (English ivy) Small-leaved, self-clinging climber that comes in an enormous range of leaf shapes and colours. Green-leaved forms are more vigorous than those with variegated foliage. Evergreen. Height 1.8–3.6m (6–12ft).

Hydrangea anomala subsp. *petiolaris* (climbing hydrangea) Self-clinging climber bearing heads of creamy-white flowers in early to mid-summer. Leaves turn yellow in autumn. Deciduous. Height 3m (10ft).

Jasminum nudiflorum (winter jasmine) Wall shrub that produces yellow flowers over a long period, often from November to March. Deciduous. Height 1.8m (6ft).

Lonicera × *tellmanniana* (honeysuckle) Twining climber that bears large showy clusters of rich yellow flowers in early to mid-summer. Unlike most honeysuckles, the blooms are not fragrant. Deciduous. Height 4m (13ft).

Large clusters of golden-yellow flowers make L. × *tellmanniana* one of the most showy honeysuckles.

how to plant a climber

1 Dig the planting hole. It must be large enough to take the roots and deep enough for the top of the rootball to come just below the surface of the ground. If you are planting against a wall, site the hole 30cm (12in) away, as bricks take moisture away from plant roots and a roof overhang keeps off rain. Work in lots of planting compost.

2 Knock the plant out of its pot and unwind any roots that are spiralling around the bottom of the rootball. Put the plant in the hole and lean it so that it touches its support. Backfill the soil around the rootball, firm gently and water well. Add a thick layer of mulch to help retain moisture.

3 Tie the stems to the support or, if the plant is self-clinging, tie them on to short bamboo canes. These will hold it secure until growth establishes.

Clematis

It's not for nothing that clematis is often called 'the queen of climbers'. The sheer quantity of different species and varieties is breathtaking. There are rampant varieties for covering large walls and sheds, well-behaved compact ones that are small enough for containers – and it's no exaggeration to say that whether you're planning to plant in full sun or shade, or something in between, there's bound to be a clematis to suit the site. Best of all, most clematis are incredibly sociable and can be planted to grow hand-over-hand through other shrubs, conifers and climbers, giving them a garland of flowers. So if you think your garden is full to the brim, clematis is the answer for more flowers. Choose a selection of types to pack your garden with colour from the start of spring through to autumn.

HYBRID OR SPECIES?

The most mouthwatering flowers belong to the large-flowered hybrid clematis that bear their plate-sized blooms in summer. Understandably, most people fall for these beauties big time, but they are a bit fussy about growing conditions. Ideally, they need a deep, moisture-retentive soil rich in organic matter and preferably neutral to alkaline rather than acid. The site should be sheltered from strong winds and they like to have their roots in the shade but their top growth in the sun.

Stop! Don't consign clematis to your list of 'can't grow' plants, for to the rescue come species clematis and these are a whole heap easier to please. Compared to the large-flowered hybrids they bear smaller flowers, but in such quantity as to give a truly stunning display and often over a longer period. They're much tougher than the hybrids and are also much less likely to suffer from clematis wilt, a disease that can result in the entire plant collapsing and dying.

LARGE-FLOWERED HYBRIDS

There are hundreds of varieties which means that every garden centre seems to offer a different selection. Most clematis have single flowers but there are some double varieties. Size, flowering time and colour are the key points to look for when choosing your clematis.

Sizes Large-flowered hybrids can be broadly divided into:
- Small: 1.8–2.4m (6–8ft)
- Medium: 2.4–4m (8–13ft)
- Large: 4–6m (13–20ft)

Small clematis are suitable for containers while larger ones need to be grown in the ground.

Flowering times Depending on the variety, hybrids flower mainly in early and mid-summer.
- Varieties that flower in early summer often have another, smaller show of blooms in late summer.
- Mid-summer varieties generally only flower once.

Colours The selection of colours is huge, ranging from whites and creams, blues and purples to pinks and reds, plus some striped in two colours.
- Paler flowers do best out of the sun as it can bleach their delicate colours.
- Brighter colours look best in sun or part shade.

Clematis are perfect for growing through other, well-established plants for a garland of extra summer colour.

pruning a clematis

1 Clematis benefit from an annual prune to avoid the plant developing a tangled mass of stems and to encourage flowers. Late winter to early spring is the time to tackle large-flowered hybrid clematis.

2 Prune each stem back to a strong pair of buds. Weak, spindly shoots should be cut back further than strong ones as this will encourage more vigorous growth.

3 Cut the stems back to different lengths, so in the summer the whole plant should be furnished with bloom from top to bottom. Tie-in stems if necessary.

SPECIES CLEMATIS

The clematis described below are easy to grow and almost guaranteed to produce a good show of flowers year after year. Only the species are listed here, but most of them have been interbred to create named hybrids that offer a wide range of colours.

Clematis alpina, C. macropetala Lovely for early spring colour. Both these clematis bear many nodding heads of semi-double to double flowers amongst divided, fresh green foliage. Suitable for growing in a large container as well as in the ground. Colours include white, blue and pink. Grow in sun or shade. Height 2.4m (8ft).

C. montana Most vigorous of all the clematis described here so make sure it has plenty of growing space. Smothered in white or pink flowers in late spring to early summer. The leaves are attractively shaped, too. Sun or part shade. Height 6m (20ft).

C. orientalis, C. tangutica These 'lantern flowered' clematis bloom from late summer to autumn and bear many nodding heads of golden or orange-yellow flowers, followed by fluffy seedheads that also look good. Sun or part shade. Height 2.4–3m (8–10ft).

C. viticella Most versatile of all the species clematis. The entire plant can be chopped back to about 45cm (18in) from the ground every winter, which means it can be grown in lots of different sites – through, and over, plants ranging from small shrubs to trees, or over sheds and other wooden structures that need painting in winter. Lots of different colours include white, pink, purple and red. Sun or part shade. Height 3m (10ft).

PLANTING A CLEMATIS

Plant a clematis in the same way that you'd plant a climber (see page 65) but with one huge difference: it should be planted deeper than it was growing previously with the top of the rootball about 7.5cm (3in) below ground level. Strong shoots will be produced from below, as well as above, the ground. This means that if the plant collapses because of clematis wilt there is a good chance it will regrow.

Clematis use twining leaf stalks to climb and do best if they are given plenty of holds to attach themselves to. Grow them on close-patterned trellis, plastic or wire mesh, or through a well-established shrub or conifer.

Choosing and growing roses

Roses tend to fall into a 'love them' or 'hate them' category so far as most people are concerned. On the plus side, they bear gorgeous, often fragrant, flowers for weeks in summer, and disease-resistant varieties need little attention. On the down side, they are prickly, dull when not in flower, and many varieties need regular spraying to combat pests and diseases.

A good compromise is to grow the occasional rose here and there around the garden, but not put all your eggs in one basket, horticulturally speaking, by having a disproportionate number of roses compared to other types of plant. That way, you'll be able to enjoy them during their flowering season, but there will be other plants to divert attention from their less pleasing qualities

at other times of the year. Also, not growing a lot of roses in one place means they will be less of a target for diseases and pests. In any case, check the plant label before you buy to see if it mentions disease resistance – many of the newer varieties, in particular, have good natural resistance and shouldn't need spraying.

WHAT DO YOU WANT IN A ROSE?
A mind-boggling selection of roses is available from specialist rose growers, but if you only want a handful of varieties a good garden centre should offer more than enough choice for your needs. Late autumn to early spring is the best time to buy and plant roses, which is when you'll find a really good selection on sale. Before you part with your cash, though, you need to know exactly what you want.

- Decide whether you prefer a rose that bears repeated flushes of flowers through the summer or a variety that produces one really spectacular display that lasts for several weeks.
- Another decision is whether to opt for modern roses with their perfect blooms or old-fashioned ones that form a mass of crumpled petals.
- Scent is another consideration. While some roses are wonderfully fragrant others are all looks but nothing else. Look at the plant description.
- Check the plant's height and spread. Don't let anyone tell you that size doesn't matter – when it comes to roses, that is. They may all look the same when they're lined up in pots at the garden centre, but get them in the ground for a couple of years and the difference will be more than plain to see. Always, but always, read the label!
- Remember that, with the exception of a few climbers which tolerate shade, most roses prefer a sunny site.

A rose around the door, like this prolifically blooming rambler 'Alberic Barbier', is many people's idea of the perfect welcome home.

ROSES FOR VERTICAL STRUCTURES

Climbing and rambling roses are both suitable for growing on walls, fences and vertical features, but to matchmake the right rose to a particular place, it's important to know the difference between the two.

Climbing roses These form a permanent framework of branches and bear flowers on sideshoots that come from these main stems. Most varieties repeat flower through the summer. They are best suited to walls, fences and trellis where the main branches need not be disturbed. For sites where there is little room for them to spread – arches, pillars and small areas of wall – choose climbers with a compact habit. The smallest of these are miniature or patio climbers which grow to around 1.8m (6ft). Where possible, train the branches fanwise or horizontally to encourage better flowering.

Rambling roses Ramblers throw out long, unruly stems and scramble over their support. They are perfect for growing over pergolas, arbours, through large trees or conifers or even over small buildings. Ramblers bear masses of small flowers in large clusters, and all but a few varieties bloom once only, in a spectacular display over several weeks.

SHRUB ROSES

Bush roses look fantastic growing alongside other plants, but only if you opt for shrub roses. These good-tempered beasts are happy to have smaller plants crowding round their heels, and will even tolerate climbers like clematis weaving through their branches. The single-flowered (hybrid tea) and cluster-flowered (floribunda) types prefer a border to themselves in order to grow well. Any underplanting should be low.

climbing roses

Miniature or patio climber roses are perfect for small spaces and can even be grown in large containers. 'Warm Welcome' makes a lovely display of glowing orange flowers.

While most climbing roses prefer a sunny site, there is a handful of varieties that will tolerate being grown in shade as well as sun. One of these is 'Golden Showers', which has double, rich yellow blooms. It has the advantage of a very long flowering season, lasting from early summer right through until autumn.

'Climbing Ena Harkness' is a wonderful old variety with beautiful deep red blooms that are strongly scented.

rambling roses

Most rambler roses bear smaller flowers than climbing roses, but in greater profusion. Their graceful stems are ideal for covering large areas. Choose a flower colour to contrast with its background, like this pure white rose 'Sander's White', against a brick wall.

Rambler roses look lovely when tumbling over a wall. One of the showiest varieties is 'Albertine', which bears coppery pink flowers that have a strong scent.

Some varieties are extremely vigorous and need to be planted where there is no need to restrict growth, like this rose 'Bobbie James'. Always check the eventual size of a variety before buying a rambler rose.

Many shrub roses are old-fashioned varieties that only have one flush of bloom – though a very spectacular one, it has to be said. However, the dainty China and Portland roses do repeat flower, as do modern shrub roses and *R. rugosa* types which are very strong, robust growers. The English roses are modern old-rose look-alikes that share the best characteristics of old and modern roses.

Size varies considerably from compact bushes that can be as little as 0.9m (3ft) high, to vigorous bushes that grow to well over twice that height.

PATIO ROSES

If you yearn for roses that are modern in appearance, but don't have much space, these are the plants to choose. These little bush roses grow to a maximum of 75cm (30in) high and are perfect for small borders and containers. The term 'patio rose' refers to dwarf bush roses that have fairly large flowers on a compact plant, as well as miniature types that have small, dainty blooms.

STANDARD ROSES

A standard rose could be described as a bush on a tall stem, and while modern varieties have a 'parks and gardens' image that puts many people off, there are all sorts of different types. Not only are standards ideal for creating some instant height, but the tall, clear stem enables lots of other plants to be grown beneath for two-tier colour. Patio standards are grown on a short stem about 60cm (24in) high and are ideal for small borders and containers, while weeping standards have an attractive trailing habit.

GROUND-COVER ROSES

So called because of their low-growing, spreading habit, ground-cover roses look grand at the edges of borders, tumbling down banks, trailing out of raised beds and even in containers. Do pick your varieties with care as they vary a lot in size. Avoid like the plague any of the large, vigorous ones as these will wrap their thorny stems around your ankles within a couple of weeks. Some good, reliable ground-cover roses to look out for include the 'County' series which are all named after the different counties of England, and the 'Flower Carpet' series. These all have a maximum spread of 90cm (36in), repeat flower well and many have good resistance to disease.

PLANTING ROSES

While roses do well on most soils, avoid soil that is very wet, chalky or peaty. They are hungry plants, so prepare the ground well by digging it to two spades' depth and working in lots of organic matter plus some slow-release fertilizer (see page 15). Autumn to early winter is the ideal time for planting both bare-root and container-grown roses, though the latter can go in at any time of the year provided they are kept well watered. Take care not to plant roses where other roses were growing previously. In particular, make sure the knobbly lump in the stem where the plant has been grafted is just above ground level.

If you are replacing old or worn-out roses with new ones try not to replant in the same spot. The diseases and viruses that attack roses are likely to have built up in the ground over the years and the new plants will never thrive. However, if you are dead set on putting the new rose in the same place as the old one, remove a 60cm (24in) cube of soil and fill the space with fresh soil from a non-rose-growing part of the garden.

CARING FOR ROSES

Prune roses every year as described on page 27. Mulch every spring to ensure that the soil is in good condition and to keep down weeds, and feed with a rose fertilizer. Cut off dead flower heads to encourage more blooms – unless the rose will also produce decorative 'hips' in the autumn.

Below: Modern ground-cover roses bear masses of flowers over a long period, and usually have a compact habit. 'Suffolk' looks delightful with deep-red blooms and contrasting golden stamens.

ground-cover roses

- 'Cheshire' (light pink, rosette shaped, spreading habit)
- 'Flower Carpet' (double, bright pink blooms, bushy)
- 'Hertfordshire' (carmine-pink, single, spreading habit)
- 'Lancashire' (cherry red, double, bushy and spreading)
- 'Suffolk' (bright scarlet with showy golden stamens, single, low and spreading)
- 'White Flower Carpet' (Double, white blooms, prostrate)
- 'Worcestershire' (Bright yellow, semi-double, prostrate)
- 'Yorkshire' (White, semi-double, bushy and spreading)

Fill the gaps

Once all the larger plants are in position, there will be plenty of gaps to pack with small shrubs, grasses and other perennials. Although these infill plants are not as big as their neighbours, they don't half pack a punch if they're chosen with a bit of care. When it comes to choosing them, the guidelines are the same as for larger plants: flowers at different times of year, good-looking foliage for summer interest and evergreens to cheer up the garden in winter. Simply select a few plants from each of the sections below and you'll be sure to have lots of colour in every season.

SPRING/EARLY SUMMER

Dicentra spectabilis (love lies bleeding) Arching stems are hung with locket-like pink-and-white flowers above fresh green foliage. Turn individual blooms upside down to see the origin of the plant's other name: 'lady in the bath'. Prefers moist soil and part shade. Height 60cm (24in).

Euphorbia Superb for bold foliage and flowers. Particularly good varieties are those such as 'Redwing' and *E. characias wulfeni* which have flower buds that look good all through winter and then bear large yellow-green flower heads in spring. Grow in sun and well-drained soil. Height 60–90cm (24–36in).

Geranium Not to be confused with frost-tender pelargoniums, which are commonly called geraniums, these hardy perennials are tough and invaluable garden plants. Choose from lots of different varieties such as 'Johnson's Blue' (sky blue); 'Rozanne' (deep blue, paler eye); 'Russell Prichard' (deep pink) and 'Wargrave Pink' (pale pink). These prefer sun or part shade, while *G. macrorrhizum* and *G. phaeum* can be grown in full shade. Height 30–60cm (12–24in).

Nepeta × *faassenii* (catmint) Aromatic grey-green leaves and blue-mauve flowers form a spreading clump that looks lovely on border edges. However, it does have a magnetic appeal for cats, so it's not a plant to grow if you're trying to keep the neighbourhood moggies out of your garden! Sun. Height 45cm (18in).

Tradescantia 'Sweet Kate' Clumps of upright, grass-like foliage are soft gold in colour, a gorgeous background to clusters of purple-blue flowers. Sun. Height 60cm (24in).

Perennials and grasses are great for infilling between larger plants and can be chosen to give colour in every season of the year. *Primula vialii* is a delightful little plant that needs a moist soil.

LATE SUMMER/AUTUMN

Aster × *frikartii* (Michaelmas daisy) Tall stems are
topped with lavender-blue, orange-centred flowers that
last for a good few weeks. While many other asters
look spectacular but then succumb to mildew, this just
looks spectacular. Grow in sun. Height 90cm (36in).

Echinops (globe thistle) An imposing plant bearing tall
'drumsticks' of metallic-blue flowers that are popular
with bees. Grow in full sun. Height 90cm (36in).

Liriope muscari (lilyturf) Evergreen perennial that bears
little 'pokers' of glowing purple flowers above rounded
clumps of grassy leaves. Great for edging. Prefers well-
drained soil in part or full shade. Height 30cm (12in).

Euphorbias are excellent for long-lasting interest, with
colourful bracts surrounding little clusters of flowers.

plants for ground cover

Spreading plants that cover the ground
are not only a great improvement on
bare soil, but they do a great job of
preventing weed growth. The scalloped
leaves and lime-green flowers of
Alchemilla mollis (lady's mantle) are
particularly good at softening the edges
of hard surfaces.

Shade-tolerant ground cover plants like
Bergenia (elephant's ears) are
tremendous for planting under trees
and large shrubs to create an extra
layer of colour. The evergreen leaves
are good for winter interest.

As well as being dense and flat-
growing, *Juniperus horizontalis*
'Montana' will tolerate both dry and
alkaline soils. It's perfect for growing in
rock gardens and on sunny banks.

make more of your perennials

When herbaceous perennials have formed established clumps they will perform better if they are dug up, divided into pieces and replanted.

Divide the plants in autumn or spring. Dig up each one and break up the clump using a spade or an old kitchen knife. Repeat the process until you have decent-sized chunks, each with several buds and plenty of root. Throw out the old, woody centre of the clump and replant the divisions.

Perennials that combine attractive foliage with flowers are very good value, like *Iris pallida* 'Variegata'.

Macleaya cordata (plume poppy) Imposing perennial that is excellent for creating rapid height. Tall stems are clad with very attractive lobed, grey-green leaves and topped with clouds of tiny buff flowers. Sun or part shade. Height to 2.4m (8ft).

Pennisetum orientale Mound-forming grass that is best in summer when the bristly flower heads fountain outwards on slender stems. Needs sun and light, well-drained soil. Height 60cm (24in).

Sedum spectabile (ice plant) Looks good over a long period with flower buds that form in mid-summer and open to large heads of long-lasting pink, purple or white flowers, attractive to bees and butterflies. Fleshy grey-green or purple-tinged leaves are also handsome. Grow in sun and well-drained soil. Height 45cm (18in).

Stipa Outstanding ornamental grasses that look spectacular when in flower. *S. gigantea* bears tall heads of open, straw-coloured flowers up to 1.8m (6ft) high, while *S. tenuissima* forms 'ponytails' of flowers on arching stems, to 60cm (24in) high. Grow in sun and well-drained soil.

WINTER/EARLY SPRING

Bergenia (elephant's ears) Large clusters of showy flowers in white, pink or purple are borne in late winter. Bold, leathery, dark green leaves make good ground cover, and the foliage of some varieties colours up in winter. Sun or shade. Height 30–45cm (12–18in).

Erica carnea (winter-flowering heather) Forms a carpet of flowers during mid-winter to early spring, depending on the variety. Unlike many heathers, which need acid soil, this type tolerates ground that is slightly alkaline (limy). Lots of varieties, in colours including white, pink, red and purple, plus a few with golden leaves. Sun or part shade. Height 15–30cm (6–12in).

Helleborus Invaluable late-winter plants with showy flowers and the added bonus of attractive evergreen foliage. *H. orientalis* (Lenten rose) bears saucer-shaped flowers in colours from pure white through pink to darkest purple. *H. foetidus* has large heads of apple-green flowers. Part or full shade. Height 45–60cm (18–24in).

SUMMER FOLIAGE

Alchemilla mollis (lady's mantle) Forms a clump of attractive fresh green leaves with lobed edges, and bears a frothy mass of greenish-yellow flowers in early summer. Sun or part shade. Height 30cm (12in).

Heuchera Rounded, colourful leaves form a neat, spreading clump of foliage. Many varieties are available, mostly in shades of purple or bronze, or mottled with silver. Slender spikes of tiny white flowers are borne in summer. Sun or part shade. Height 45cm (18in).

Hosta Fantastic foliage plants in a range of colours including gold, green-and-white and blue-grey. Hostas need a moist soil and shelter from cold winds. Slugs and snails tend to munch the leaves to ribbons, and growing the plants in containers is sometimes the only resort. Part or full shade. Height 30–60cm (12–24in).

Iris pallida **'Variegata'** Upright, sword-shaped leaves are bright green striped with creamy yellow. Soft blue flowers are produced in early summer. Grow on well-drained soil in sun. Height 45cm (18in).

Polemonium **'Brise d'Anjou'** Small, rounded, bright green leaves are boldly edged with white. Stems of blue flowers borne in summer contrast beautifully with the foliage. Sun or part shade. Height 60cm (24in).

Stachys byzantina **'Silver Carpet'** (lamb's ears) Spreading plant with slender, woolly, silvery leaves that are irresistible to touch. Needs well-drained soil and sun. Height 30cm (12in).

EVERGREEN FOLIAGE

Carex oshimensis **'Evergold'** (sedge) A neat, low mound of slender, gold-striped leaves that looks lovely all year. Grow in sun or part shade. Height 30cm (12in).

Euonymus fortunei Tough evergreen shrubs that are invaluable for ground cover and winter interest, particularly those with variegated leaves, like 'Emerald Gaiety', 'Emerald 'n' Gold' and 'Harlequin'. Grow in sun or shade, on any reasonably well-drained soil. Height to 45cm (18in).

Make sure that you leave enough space between plants when positioning them. Look at the label to get information on height and spread and plant accordingly.

Euphorbia amygdaloides **var.** *robbiae* Dark green rosettes of leaves form wide, spreading clumps. Stems of yellow-green 'flowers' are produced in spring. Invaluable plant for difficult, shady places. Sun or shade. Height 45cm (18in).

Festuca glauca (blue fescue) Ornamental grass that forms small, rounded clumps of thin, blue-grey leaves. Grow in sun and well-drained soil. Height 30cm (12in).

Vinca minor (lesser periwinkle) Carpet-forming plant with glossy leaves and spring flowers. Leaves are plain green, green-and-white or gold-and-green, and flowers are white, blue or purple. Take care not to plant the thuggish *Vinca major* (greater periwinkle) unless you want to cover a large area! Sun or shade. Height 15cm (6in).

WHEN TO PLANT PERENNIALS

The ideal time for planting perennials is early autumn or spring, but they can be put in during summer, provided they are kept well watered during dry spells. Plant as for shrubs (page 57).

Seasonal spectaculars

While permanent plants may be the stalwarts of a garden, there's nothing to beat the party animals of the plant world – those that create an absolute riot of colour for a short time. Bulbs pop out of the ground to do their stuff from January through to the summer months, then disappear until next year. Biennials flower in later spring or early summer, after which they will be chucked on the compost heap. Hardy annuals make a fantastic display over a couple of months, while half-hardy annuals and frost-tender perennials flower their socks off from early summer until they are clobbered by the first frosts of autumn.

The fun part of growing short-lived flowers is that you can have something different every year – maybe tasteful pastel shades one year followed by a vivid bonanza of eye-socking colours the next. There's no need to go short of flowers even if you're on a tight budget as masses of plants can be grown from just a few pounds' worth of seed.

BULBS FOR EARLY COLOUR

There's a huge range of bulbs on sale, and while it's tempting to try lots of different ones you'll create a better effect by planting larger quantities of just a few varieties. Choose bulbs that flower at different times in order to have a glorious succession of colour from late winter right through to early summer. The show starts in January and February with snowdrops and winter aconites, moves on to the first narcissi, then kicks into gear big time with a wealth of daffodils, narcissi, tulips, hyacinths and many others, finishing with late-flowering varieties of tulips and narcissi in May.

PLANTING BULBS

Even the least green-fingered gardener will find it hard to go wrong with bulbs. They contain their own store of energy, so you're almost guaranteed a good show for a year or two, and usually for a lot longer. Just remember these four vital points for success.

make bulb planting easy

Many people like to plant sizable groups of bulbs to achieve a really stunning final effect, but planting in large numbers can be hard work. Although a standard, short-handled bulb-planter that takes out a core of the soil is easier to use than a trowel, a long-handled one could save a lot of wear and tear on your planting arm and be a worthwhile investment in the long term.

Bulbs are absolutely unbeatable for making a superb show of spring colour that really lifts the spirits after a long, gloomy winter.

planting snowdrop bulbs in grass

1 Brighten up your lawn in winter by planting some snowdrops. Use a spade to cut a flap of turf out of the lawn, and roll it back to reveal the soil.

2 Dig out 7.5cm (3in) of soil and place the bulbs in small groups for a natural-looking appearance.

3 Replace the soil, firm it gently and roll back the turf. Remember to let the bulb foliage die back naturally after flowering to ensure a good display the next year. When your clump of bulbs gets overcrowded, dig them up about six weeks after flowering, divide and replant.

- Plant bulbs at the depth suggested on the packet. It refers to the depth of the soil on top of the bulb. If your bulbs come without instructions, a good rule of thumb is to plant bulbs three times deeper than their height.
- Plant them at the right time. Early-flowering bulbs like snowdrops and crocus, plus all daffodils and narcissi, should be in the ground by the end of September because they need lots of time to make root growth. Hold off planting tulips until October and November, as they tend to rot if planted earlier.
- Plant them in the right place – basically anywhere except in soggy soil. Spring bulbs can be grown almost anywhere in the garden, including under trees and large deciduous shrubs – the bulbs will be over and done before the permanent plants leaf up and take all the light. Bulbs can also be planted in grass, provided you'll be able to hold off mowing for

six weeks while their leaves die back after flowering. They can also go almost anywhere in a border as they'll be able to wiggle their shoots through to the light.

- Once flowering has finished, remove the dead flower heads on large bulbs, but leave them on in the case of bulbs like snowdrops or bluebells, so they can self-seed. The leaves must be allowed to die back naturally so the bulb can build up energy for next year.

The only problem is that, come bulb-planting time, the garden tends to be packed with plants and it's hard to imagine – let alone get to – the right places for the bulbs. The solution is to plant them in the plastic pots that shrubs are grown in – the chances are a friend will have some even if you haven't – and when spring arrives you just plant out your almost-flowering bulbs into exactly the right spots.

See also 'Beautiful bulbs' (pages 92–3) and 'Instant bulbs for borders' (page 40).

GROWING BIENNIALS

Biennials are often called spring bedding plants because varieties like *Cheiranthus* (wallflower) and *Bellis* (double daisy) make a spectacular show along with bulbs. However, others like *Digitalis purpurea* (foxglove) and *Hesperis matrionalis* (sweet rocket) are lovely, easy flowers for the border in early summer.

Biennials grow from seed sown in summer and are planted out in autumn to flower the following year. It's dead easy to grow them from seed if you have a spare corner of ground in which to sow a few rows, or you'll find a good selection of plants on sale in garden centres in autumn. When the plants have flowered, dig them up and compost them or, if you like the informal cottage-garden look, leave them until the seed pods have turned brown and scattered the ripe seeds so that they grow of their own accord for next spring.

Foxgloves are easy biennials to grow and their tall spires of flowers make attractive border displays.

how to sow a border of hardy annuals

1 Choose a sunny spot in the garden, then dig over the soil and rake it to break up any lumps. Use a bamboo cane to trace patches in the soil for the different plants, marking them clearly by sprinkling sand along their edges.

2 Use the cane to draw out several shallow lines, or seed drills, within each patch. The lines should be about 1cm (½in) deep. Sow the seed thinly, rake a little soil over them, and firm the soil gently with the back of the rake. You can sow in autumn on light, sandy soils, or in spring on heavier ground.

3 Finally, label the different patches, water the seeds in and lay twigs across to deter cats. Water again when dry.

HARDY ANNUALS: THE EASIEST OPTION

If you've never grown anything from seed before, start with hardy annuals. There's no need for any special equipment as seed can be sown straight into the ground (see box, opposite). Hardy annuals are great for new gardens because they can be used to fill the gaps between newly planted permanent plants, and also look fantastic on their own in a border. Although the blooms won't last as long as those of half-hardy annuals and frost-tender perennials, you'll have a good couple of months of colour for little money and effort.

TENDER PLANTS FOR SUMMER COLOUR

Nothing beats a riot of summer flowers at the time of year when you're outside enjoying your garden. Half-hardy annuals and frost-tender perennials will put on a show for months, and the results are well worth the time and money.

It used to be fashionable to plant up or 'bed out' entire borders with these tender summer plants – hence their other name 'bedding plants' – but most people now prefer to have a fair number of permanent

Pots of half-hardy annuals and tender perennials bring colour to the garden when they can be most appreciated.

plants for all-year interest and lower maintenance. Have the best of both worlds and leave a few spaces for half-hardy annuals and tender perennials within your borders. These short-lived plants are also ideal in pots (see pages 86–7). While the majority are sun-lovers a few, such as fuchsias and lobelia, prefer partial shade.

There are stacks of different plants so it's worth ordering a few free seed catalogues to browse through at your leisure in winter.

WAIT TO BED OUT TENDER PLANTS

Patience is the watchword if you want to be sure of a successful display. The terms 'half-hardy' and 'frost-tender' mean the plants are likely to be damaged or killed by even a light frost. Although garden centres have them on sale from early spring, don't buy and plant outside until all danger of frost is past. This varies according to the part of the country you live in – mid May in the mild south and early June in the north.

CONTAINER GARDENING

The basics

You'll never be bored with a display of pots. Containers are ideally suited to stage management and can be moved around to create a fresh look in minutes. Any that become scruffy can simply be thrown out or whisked out of sight to recover or await replanting. First though, you need to choose your containers and decide where to put them and how to display them.

Use containers to make the most of every available site in the garden. The fragrance of hyacinths and narcissi can be fully appreciated on this flight of steps.

CHOOSING CONTAINERS

There's a vast range of containers on sale, in different sizes and in materials like terracotta, stone, wood, plastic and metal – plus hanging baskets, window boxes, freestanding pots on legs (the posh name is *jardinière*) and all sorts of growing bags. Be wary, though, of falling into the common trap of buying a bit of everything and ending up with a real mixed bag of pots. For a really stylish look it can be helpful to choose a theme for your containers and plants. Terracotta pots, for example, give a Mediterranean feel, or paint your pots in two or three complementary colours to bring a real sense of unity to a miscellaneous collection.

Cost is an obvious factor when it comes to selecting containers, particularly if you're planning on a plethora of pots. However, you needn't spend a penny if you adapt different throwaway items. Anything that holds compost and can have drainage holes put into it can be planted up. Potential containers include old hot water cylinders (cut in half with a hacksaw), old sinks, mop buckets and even chimney pots topped with a large flower pot. If you're not great at DIY, why not have a go at making your own wooden containers? You could even make a matching set if you find you've got a talent in this direction. Remember that a coat of paint and a few trailing plants can conceal a good few mistakes!

POSITIONING POTS

Pots can be placed virtually anywhere, but to position them to the best effect it pays to look at your garden from both indoors and out. Obvious places for concentrations of containers are the patio, any other seating areas and around the front door for a flowery welcome home. Include a few fragrant plants in these spots. Wafts of scent are part and parcel of a garden. While containers will be enjoyed outside for a good part of the year, don't forget that our variable climate dictates that for the greater part you're likely to be indoors looking out. So for autumn, winter and early spring, move a good proportion of pots to where they can be seen from inside the house.

Containers are the only way to bring colour to places where there is no soil at all, like the paving or concrete between a house and a fence or garage wall. Large pots like wooden half-barrels can be used here for substantial plants like climbers and shrubs which will work full-time to soften the hard lines of the wall or fence.

Pots also make good focal points. Look for the key viewpoints such as at the end of a path or the view from the main windows in the house. Siting handsome pots in places like these gives the eye something to focus on and creates good structure within the garden. If a bit of background scenery can be 'borrowed', so much the better – established shrubs in the border will make a good backdrop to offset the pots, or a coloured fence will provide an effective contrast.

PLANTS FOR ALL SEASONS

The most popular plants for containers are short-lived bedding or patio plants that look supremely colourful right through the summer months until they're killed off by autumn frosts. However, a huge and varied range of other plants can also be grown in containers, including bulbs, shrubs, climbers, conifers, perennials and ornamental grasses. With all these topnotch plants at your disposal, it's easy to have a potted garden that looks great through every month of the year. There are even edible plants like herbs, fruit and vegetables to provide a potted feast into the bargain.

When it comes to shady and sunny sites, be sure to match the right plant to the right place. Most seasonal summer varieties prefer a fair amount of sun to do well, but there are plenty of permanent plants to cheer up a spot in the shade.

MIXING AND MATCHING

Pots can be planted up with just one variety of plant or several different plants can be combined in one

Containers can be filled with colour for every season of the year. Tulips and grape hyacinths make a glorious show of spring flowers.

medium to large container. The simplest approach, particularly if you're new to gardening, is to stick to single-plant pots and juggle them around until you're happy with the results.

For a really good-looking display, it's best to group containers rather than scattering individual ones around the garden. Introduce a change of levels to make them look really attractive – sit two or three pots on top of each other, on upturned pots or on a small stack of bricks. Add even more height at the back with a container-grown climber trained up a support (see page 95). For guaranteed good looks, use a selection of pots in the same material but in different shapes and sizes. If you already have a lot of different containers, separate them out so that there's one group of terracotta, one of glazed pots and another of wooden troughs, for example.

Limiting the mixture of plants in a group of containers will look much better than if you plant a jumble of different ones. To be ultra-effective, have a go at creating a colour scheme such as blue and yellow; pink, blue and silver; or orange and yellow. Many garden centres sell summer-flowering plants according to colour, which makes the choice a lot easier.

CARING FOR PLANTS IN POTS

Plants in containers are a bit like pets – they rely on you for all their needs and can't be left to their own devices for any length of time at all. Follow these top tips to have glorious container displays.

- Always scrub out used containers before replanting in them as old compost and plant material can harbour pests and diseases. Use hot water and a stiff brush.
- Always use fresh potting compost (see page 13).
- Avoid watering in the heat of the day when more water is lost by evaporation and when water-splashed growth can become sun-scorched.

A single plant in an attractive container can be moved around the garden to make a striking focal point.

set up a drip system

The daily routine of watering your containers in summer may be relaxing but it can be a real pain if you're away on holiday or just rushed off your feet. Set up a drip system complete with timer and your plants will be taken care of whether you're home or away. The system consists of a large pipe, which runs around the area to be watered, with thinner pipes, each of which waters a single pot, coming from it.

- Stand your containers exactly where you want them, then measure the distance between them and your tap and count the number of pots to calculate what you will need in the way of materials.
- Run the main pipe where it will be least obvious – at the base of a wall or fence, for example. If you're making a system for hanging baskets, run the pipe in a straight

line between the ground and first-floor windows. Use joints to fit it snugly around corners.

- Open the tap just enough for the water to flow through the pipes and drip into the containers.
- Pierce holes in the main pipe and insert the smaller pipes into them, then fit drip heads to the ends of the smaller pipes and peg each one into a container.

Set up the system in hot weather, when the pipes are more flexible. It will also be easier to fit the joints and drip heads if you dip the ends of smaller pipes into a pan of hot water.

Before the onset of winter make sure the pipes are drained of water which could otherwise freeze and damage them. Ideally, dismantle the system and store it until the weather warms up again.

making a raised bed

1 A raised bed is very similar to a container for growing plants. Make your own simple raised bed using pieces of 150 × 50mm (6 × 2in) pressure-treated or tanalized timber.

2 Check that the corners are at exact right angles. If you want to build a taller raised bed, make another frame in the same way for the next layers, but with the joints overlapping. For extra support, add an upright to each internal corner of the bed and screw-fix each one into place.

3 Drill a couple of holes at each join and secure with screws. Put your raised bed in position and put a layer of broken pots or large stones in the base for drainage.

- Regular watering is vital and may even be necessary when it rains as the soil in a pot is usually shielded by an 'umbrella' of foliage. Sunny, breezy weather will dry plants out really fast and in such conditions watering may be required twice a day.
- Aim to keep the compost evenly moist so that it doesn't dry out or become waterlogged.
- Install a drip system (see box, opposite).
- Feeding is necessary from spring to late summer. Start about six weeks after putting the plants in the pot, when the fertilizer in the potting compost has been used up. Choose between weekly applications of liquid fertilizer or a one-off dose of controlled-release fertilizer (see page 16–17).

Regular watering is essential to keep pot-grown plants healthy, as the soil is shielded by a canopy of foliage that stops rain reaching the roots.

Summer containers

Bedding or patio plants – correctly known as half-hardy annuals and tender perennials – are great in containers as they bloom continuously from early or mid-summer right through until the first frosts. And flower-filled pots make a garden look really inviting, creating the perfect atmosphere regardless of whether you want to relax on the patio or have some friends round for a barbecue.

USE SHAPES AND FOLIAGE

For a really effective summer show it's worth splashing out and buying one or two really large containers and using them with small and medium ones to create a bit of 'oomph'. The beauty of big pots is that they can house one large permanent plant as a centrepiece – a spiky-leaved Cordyline or a bay tree trimmed into a lollipop shape – which can be planted round with a mass of summer flowers like geraniums, impatiens

(busy lizzies) or petunias. Its bold, architectural shape will offset the flowers to perfection.

If you're planting up a pot solely with summer-flowering plants, put the larger, bushy ones like argyranthemum (marguerites) or geraniums in the centre and surround them with smaller plants with a more open, lax habit – diascias, impatiens (busy lizzies) and verbenas, for example. Include plants with attractive foliage to provide a contrast to the flowers. Good ones include *Helichrysum petiolare* with silver, lime-yellow or variegated leaves, and trailing ivies with green or variegated leaves. While most summer plants are sun lovers, fuchsias prefer partial shade. Keep a look out for *Fuchsia* 'Charlie Dimmock'!

BE RUTHLESS!

Bedding and patio plants sometimes run out of steam towards the end of the summer, particularly if they've been under stress because of a lack of food or water. If this happens, don't prolong the agony. Chuck them out and replace them with a few dahlias and chrysanthemums which will flower their socks off from late summer right through the autumn.

SUMMER CLIMBERS

Annual climbers are wonderful in large pots placed where they can be trained up an obelisk, a wigwam of canes or an adjacent wall or fence. Most garden centres stock young plants of sweet peas, which make a superb show of colourful, scented flowers. Larger centres may stock plants like *Ipomoea tricolor* (morning glory) which has large flowers of an incredibly beautiful shade of sky blue. Dead easy to grow from seed are *Tropaeolum majus* (nasturtium) and *T. peregrinum* (canary creeper).

If a container doesn't have drainage holes, then make some. Otherwise water builds up inside and plant roots will die when deprived of air.

PLANTING A CONTAINER

Good drainage is essential, so first check that the drainage holes in your container are clear. Then put a 5cm (2in) layer of material like broken pieces of terracotta pot, large stones or chunks of polystyrene on the base.

Put some potting compost in the container and dig holes for the plants. These should be wide enough and deep enough to take all the roots. Put the largest plants in first, sitting them so that the tops of their rootballs are about 3cm (1in) below the rim of the container. Add a bit more compost, put in the smaller plants and fill the spaces between the plants with compost, firming it very gently with your fingers. Finally, water thoroughly with a watering can fitted with a rose. If the compost sinks and leaves gaps, fill these in and water again.

WHEN TO PLANT

Whatever you do, avoid putting bedding plants outside until late spring as they will be killed or severely checked if they are exposed to frost. The trouble is, garden centres tend to stock them early in the year and many people are misled into planting too soon. There'll be no lack of choice if you wait until the right planting time, so don't be tempted to buy beforehand unless you have a greenhouse or conservatory in which to grow the plants.

All tender plants are raised under cover and it's best to acclimatize them gradually to the outside world over a couple of weeks, a process known as 'hardening off'. A cold frame is ideal for this as it can be opened or shut as required, but the same effect can be achieved with a bit more work by standing plants outside for increasing periods. Leave them out during the day to begin with, then all night provided the weather isn't severe.

'STARTER' PLANTS

Buying ready-grown plants in early summer can be fairly costly, but from late winter to early spring garden centres stock an excellent range of 'starter' or 'plug' plants. These well-rooted young plants are ready to pot up into 8cm (3in) pots, and could save you a fair bit of cash provided you have somewhere under cover where you can grow them on, like a sunny window sill, a heated greenhouse or a conservatory.

top 10 plants for summer pots

- *Argyranthemum*
- *Chrysanthemum*
- *Dahlia*
- **Fuchsia*
- *Impatiens*
- *Nemesia*
- **Pelargonium* (geranium)
- **Petunia*
- *Solenopsis*
- **Verbena*

* = available in trailing as well as bushy varieties

Tender perennials like this beautiful white *Argyranthemum* (marguerite) will flower right through the summer.

BASKETS AND BAGS

As gardens become smaller and space is increasingly precious, often the only way to get more plants into a garden is to go up. Lots of different containers can be fixed directly on to walls and fences, or hung from brackets, to bring vibrant colour to the dullest spots. Containers like these are brilliant for transforming areas with no ground space at all, such as the front of a house. Hanging baskets come in several designs, materials and sizes.

Baskets made from plastic-coated wire mesh These are the cheapest and, good news, they look really great as they can be planted through the sides as well as the top to create a globe of glorious colour. Such open-mesh baskets need liners in a matching size.

Solid plastic baskets These are also cheap, but the plastic is unslightly and needs to be completely hidden with trailing plants.

Baskets made from rattan They look really good – the rattan is a bit like heavy-duty wicker – but cost more.

Wall baskets and mangers Flat on one side, they can be fixed directly on to a wall. Like the mesh baskets, they also need lining.

All the above must be suspended from metal brackets. Be sure to fix the brackets and baskets very securely, as all containers are fairly weighty when wet. Use plastic wall plugs when putting screws into walls.

The following variations on the basket theme are also useful if you're planning to create a hanging garden:

Wall pots These can be hung from hooks or nails on either walls or fences.

Flower pouches Easy, cheap and effective, a flower pouch is basically a tough plastic growing bag that can be hung from a single hook or nail. To look really good it must be packed with plants so that the plastic is completely hidden. Small 'starter' or 'plug' plants are

Hanging baskets made of wire mesh are the most versatile, as plants can be put through the sides for extra colour.

the best kind to use as only small slits are needed for inserting the rootballs. Choose those with a spreading or trailing habit, like impatiens (busy lizzie) and trailing lobelia.

Where most people go wrong is that they hang the pouch up at once with the result that a sort of landslide takes place inside it. It is important to leave the pouch lying down for several weeks until the plants are well rooted and not to hang it up before then.

Security Unfortunately, these hanging containers are sometimes stolen from the front of houses. Avoid this by attaching them firmly to their support using wire or even a small padlock.

SUMMER PLANTS FOR BASKETS

Trailing plants will give colour all summer – select them for their attractive foliage as well as their flowers. Either put several plants of the same type in one container, or be adventurous and try a mixed planting. Avoid using trailing petunias with other plants as they are ultravigorous and tend to overwhelm any close neighbours.

For a mixed basket, choose up to three or four different types of flowering plant. Put one to three bushy types like impatiens (busy lizzie), pelargoniums (geraniums) or petunias in the centre, and plant a trailer like bidens, brachyscome, lobelia or scaevola around the edges and, if applicable, through the sides of the basket. Include some plants with attractive foliage, like *Glechoma hederacea* 'Variegata' (ground ivy), *Lysimachia nummularia* 'Aurea' (golden creeping Jenny) and plectranthus (Swedish ivy), which will show up the flowering plants to perfection. Don't be tempted to skimp on the number of plants you use. Baskets, particularly open-mesh types, look best when they're crammed full.

PLANTING AN OPEN-MESH BASKET

Line the basket with a suitable liner and sit it over an empty bucket for stability. Put a little compost in the base and, starting at the bottom and working upwards, plant through the sides, making holes in the liner where necessary. Depending on whether a plant's rootballs are small or large, either push the rootball in from outside or gently pull the plant through from inside. Plant round the basket, alternating different varieties. Add more compost as you go.

Continue until the compost comes within a couple of centimetres of the rim. Now place the plants with a short, bushy habit in the centre of the top layer. Hang the basket up and gently water it.

WINDOW BOXES

Window boxes will allow you to enjoy your container plants from indoors as well as out. If your window sills aren't large enough to support them, don't worry. The boxes can be fixed to stout shelf brackets that are screwed firmly to the outside wall. In any event, this is a wise precaution to take for any box above ground-floor level, as it could do someone a nasty injury if it fell. Use plants that are naturally short in habit like pansies, violas, diascia and nemesia, along with some of the trailing ones described left and below.

Below: A window box can be placed on a broad sill, or fixed to a pair of brackets if the sill is too narrow.

top 10 trailing plants for summer

- *Bidens*
- *Brachyscome*
- *Fuchsia
- Ivy-leaved *pelargonium*
- *Lobelia
- *Petunia
- *Scaevola*
- *Sutera*
- *Torrenia*
- *Verbena

*= plants come in upright as well as trailing varieties, so be sure to choose the right ones.

Autumn and winter colour

Many people send their containers to the shed for a long winter holiday, but as the temperature starts to fall there are still plenty of hardy performers to keep them looking lovely. Autumn and winter containers can be even more rewarding than summer ones as a few bright plants will really cheer up gloomy days.

Start with autumn-flowering plants that will last into winter, plus a range of hardy bedding plants that will bring interest into the shortening days. Combine these with winter-flowering plants or attractive foliage ones. Tuck in a few bulbs when planting your container, and there'll be a bonanza of blooms to herald the spring.

Shapely evergreens, like this dainty little standard *Buxus sempervirens* (box) come into their own in the winter when flowers are in short supply.

AUTUMN FLOWERS AND FOLIAGE

Several plants make a cracking display until the temperature really plummets. Cyclamen – the kind sold as house plants – carry a colourful show of flowers in many shades of white, pink, red and purple. Winter cherry, with its bright display of glossy orange berries, is also worth liberating from the house-plant category. For contrast, combine them with the half-hardy heather *Erica gracilis*, which has a choice of white, pale pink or crimson flowers. All these plants are relatively short-lived and won't tolerate much in the way of frost, but will brighten up most, if not all, of your autumn if they're tucked into a sheltered spot. They won't cost more than a decent bunch of cut flowers and will last a lot longer.

Ornamental cabbages and kale are fun and extremely effective, with frilled leaves that are variegated in white, pink and purple. Don't try to eat them though – the taste is not to be recommended. Although frost hardy, they tend to become tatty later in winter and are best used just for autumn.

BERRIES AND BLOOMS

Add 'zing' to autumn containers with *Skimmia japonica* subsp. *reevesiana* or *Gaultheria procumbens*, which bear berries of sealing-wax red that last for months – often into winter – and are handsomely evergreen into the bargain. Both need lime-free (ericaceous) compost.

Winter-flowering pansies are bedded out in autumn and will bloom on and off for months on end – all the more so if they are deadheaded regularly. While flowering tends to halt in severe weather, it soon picks up again with a bit of sun.

EVERGREENS: A WINTER BONUS

Evergreen shrubs turn into prima donnas in winter when there is a huge shortage of good-looking plants. Golden-leaved types like aucuba, elaeagnus, euonymus and ilex (holly) bring a ray of sunshine to the dullest days, while the white-and-green leaves of other hollies and *Viburnum tinus* 'Variegatum' lighten any gloomy spots. Trailing evergreens like ivies and *Vinca minor* (lesser periwinkle) look great tumbling out of pots and raised beds.

Conifers are second to none. Not only do they come in wonderful variations of gold, green and blue, but their shapes are also attractive. A collection in

---

top 10 evergreens for winter

- *Aucuba japonica* 'Crotonifolia'
- *Buxus sempervirens*
- *Elaeagnus* 'Gilt Edge'
- *Euonymus japonicus* varieties with variegated foliage
- *Euonymus fortunei* varieties with variegated foliage
- *Hebe albicans* varieties
- *Ilex* (holly) varieties with coloured/variegated foliage
- *Sarcococca*
- *Skimmia japonica* 'Rubella'
- *Viburnum tinus* 'Eve Price'

---

contrasting colours, in different shapes like upright, spreading, mound-forming and pyramidal, is outstanding. However, do take care and only choose dwarf varieties that will be happy in pots. Conifers are a bit like puppies – they all look cute when tiny, but some can turn into monsters.

Among the best evergreens are those like the *Viburnum tinus* varieties that do a double whammy of flowers plus evergreen foliage. Some, like sarcococca (Christmas box) and skimmia also have scented flowers.

PLANTING AND CARE

Plant up the containers following the guidelines on page 87, but take particular care over the drainage as plants could be killed if the compost becomes soggy and freezes. Choose well-grown plants and place them closely together so that they look well established from the start, as very little growing is done in autumn and winter. During very cold spells, protect plants by moving the containers under cover.

how to plant a hanging basket for winter colour

1 Line the basket with a liner and stand it on a pot. Put a little hanging basket compost in the base. Plant several trailing plants through the sides by gently pulling the stems through the mesh, or by pushing the rootball in from outside.

2 Put in more trailing plants, filling with compost as you go, then put in bushy plants around the top of the basket.

3 Firm the compost gently to fill the gaps between plants, but take care not to over-firm it. Hang the basket up before watering it using a can fitted with a fine rose.

Beautiful bulbs

Bulbs are second to none for providing vivid spring colour and will liven up your pots like nothing else at this time of year. Choose varieties that flower at different times so that you have 'spring' bulbs from late winter through to early summer, then lilies for summer colour. Bulbs are virtually foolproof as all their energy is stored within, so you're pretty well guaranteed a good show for the first year at least.

SIGNS OF SPRING

The very first bulbs are a real tonic. Little daffodils like 'January Gold' and 'February Gold' are a sign that winter is coming to an end, and the earliest species of crocus in February are followed in March by the larger, showier Dutch crocus. Tulips start to appear in earnest in early spring, with the Kaufmanniana types among the first showy varieties.

A CONTINUOUS DISPLAY

Tulips and narcissi create an amazing pageant of colour but the vast range of varieties to choose from can make your head spin. They flower over a very long period, so choose varieties that bloom at different times in order to have colour right into early summer. For growing in containers, it's best to pick out varieties that look really good for as long as possible, which often means paying a bit extra. For example, the little multiflowered daffodils called narcissi are more expensive than large trumpet-flowered varieties, but they last longer and are often scented into the bargain. The best tulips for pots are those which are real exhibitionists, either multiheaded with several flowers per stem or the Greigii tulip varieties which have prettily striped or patterned leaves. Hyacinths are superb in pots and their large, showy flowers have a wonderfully strong perfume.

LUSCIOUS LILIES FOR SUMMER

With their huge flowers borne on tall stems, lilies can be slotted into virtually any group of pots to stand head and shoulders above their neighbours. Not only do the flowers look exotic but they're great for creating height. Even better, quite a few varieties, particularly Regal and Oriental lilies, are deliciously scented. As with spring bulbs, choose varieties that bloom at different times so

top 10 bulbs for colour

- *Crocus* 'Saturnus'
- *Narcissus* 'February Gold'
- *Tulipa* 'Stresa'
- *Narcissus* 'Hawera'
- *Tulipa* 'Red Riding Hood'
- *Hyacinthus* 'Delft Blue'
- *Narcissus* 'Quail'
- *Tulipa* 'Georgette'
- *Lilium regale*
- *Lilium orientale* 'Kyoto'

Golden narcissi and blue hyacinths.

how to plant bulbs in layers

1 Choose a large, fairly deep container. Put in drainage material and a layer of compost. Put in the largest bulbs, such as daffodils, so they will be covered with almost 15cm (6in) of compost.

2 Cover this first layer of bulbs with compost and add the medium-sized bulbs, such as tulips. As a rough guide, you should use 10 each of the medium and large bulbs and 20 small ones.

3 Cover with compost and plant the smallest bulbs, such as crocus, then cover these with about 5cm (2in) of compost.

that you have flowers right through the season. Plant them in large pots (at least 30cm/12in across) and put in 3–5 bulbs per pot as single lilies look lost and lonely.

WHEN TO PLANT BULBS

Plant bulbs that flower in spring between August and November, depending on the variety. Early-flowering bulbs, plus all daffodils and narcissi, should be planted by the end of September. Tulips are best put in during October or November as they may rot if this is done earlier. Lilies should be planted in early to mid-spring.

PLANTING BULBS IN CONTAINERS

Good drainage is the key to success when growing bulbs in containers. This applies particularly to spring-flowering ones, as they are likely to rot if they sit for weeks in cold, soggy compost. So make sure the pots have plenty of drainage holes, and put a good layer of drainage material like broken pieces of pot, stones or chunks of polystyrene on the base.

Use any general-purpose potting compost except those that contain water-retaining granules as they'll be too wet in winter. Plant the bulbs at the depth recommended on the packet – this refers to the amount of soil over the top of the bulb.

Stand the containers in a sheltered spot like the base of a house wall over winter. If you have an unheated conservatory, greenhouse or cold frame, so much the better.

AFTER FLOWERING – WHAT THEN?

Bulbs can give repeat displays for years if they are looked after. Cut off dead flower heads and keep the plants well watered, adding liquid feed on two or three occasions, until the leaves have yellowed and died, which is how bulbs build up energy for the next year. If you need the pots for other plants, take the bulbs out and store them for replanting in autumn. Leave lilies undisturbed apart from top-dressing them in early spring, as for permanent plants (see page 95).

Low-maintenance containers

For spectacular container gardens that last for years with very little work on your part, either grow only permanent plants or those that can be surrounded by seasonal ones for extra colour. The key to success lies in choosing the right plants for the job – in this case, naturally small varieties of shrubs, conifers, roses, herbaceous perennials, ornamental grasses and climbers – all of which must look good for a long period of time if they are to be worthy of a site in your pots.

FOCUS ON FOLIAGE

Foliage plants offer a vast range of leaf shapes and colours and have the huge bonus of looking lovely for at least half the year – all year round in the case of evergreens. Colourful leaves also make a superb contrast to flowering plants as well as looking gorgeous in their own right. Some plants respond well

to trimming and can be made into decorative shapes, or topiary (see page 61).

- Large, spiky-leaved plants like *Cordyline australis* (cabbage tree), phormium (New Zealand flax) and yucca look extremely dramatic. The most attractive varieties are those with coloured rather than green leaves. Site them in a sunny, sheltered spot where the sharp leaf tips will be well away from passers-by, and watch your eyes when weeding!
- Ornamental grasses and bamboos offer a wealth of foliage colours and range from 30-cm (12-in) dwarfs to substantial specimens that top 1.8m (6ft). Extra-pleasing is their tendency to sway and rustle in the slightest breeze, bringing life and drama to the patio.
- Hostas are the top perennials for pots, partly because their large, bold leaves are so good at brightening shady corners, and also because if they are in containers they are more protected against the slugs and snails that turn their luscious leaves into lace curtains.

RHODODENDRONS AND ROSES

Containers make it possible to grow lime-hating plants even in soil that doesn't suit them. Rhododendrons, azaleas, pieris and camellias all make a glorious show of spring flowers, but take care to search out compact varieties like *Rhododendron yakushimanum* hybrids and Japanese azaleas that are suitable for pots. Grow them in ericaceous or lime-free potting compost.

Summer is the glory time for roses and several types are ideal for pots, notably miniatures, patio roses, many ground-cover varieties and miniature standards. Look for the key words 'repeat flowering' and 'disease resistant' on plant descriptions in order to achieve the best possible performance with the minimum of work.

Climbing plants, like ivies, can be trained on frames to create attractive and unusual container plants.

CLIMBERS

Climbers that are compact by nature make an unusual container display. Many clematis are suitable, although they do prefer to have their roots in the shade if they are to perform at their best. Choose compact summer-flowering hybrids like 'Arctic Queen', 'Arabella', 'Pink Champagne' and 'Sunset', and the spring-flowering species *C. alpina* and *C. macropetala*. There are also miniature climbing roses that grow to around 1.8m (6ft) and need a large container like a half-barrel. *Hedera helix* (ivy) varieties are great for training on wire frames to make quick and economical topiary shapes.

PLANTING UP PERMANENT PLANTS

Plant up following the guidelines on page 91. Use a frost-proof container and fill it with a soil-based potting compost, unless weight is an issue. If it is, use a soil-less type. If the container is large, pot it up on its final site, or mount the pot on casters to make moving it easier. Put in one permanent plant per pot, and add seasonal flowers if desired.

CARING FOR PERMANENT PLANTS

During very cold spells, the danger to watch out for is that the roots of the plants may freeze solid. This applies particularly to evergreens which can die of thirst as their leaves continue to lose water.

Move containers into a sheltered spot against a house wall over winter and stand them close together. Wrap their pots in bubble polythene if the weather is horrendously cold. Evergreens can be given extra protection with a layer of horticultural fleece, an ultralight fabric with good insulating properties, over the polythene. The fleece is readily available from garden centres or by post. Alternatively, an unheated structure, such as a porch, greenhouse or conservatory, provides ideal protection for plants.

Every spring, give the plants a boost by top-dressing them – replacing 2.5–5cm (1–2in) of compost from the top of the pot with fresh potting compost mixed with a controlled-release fertilizer. Alternatively, pot them up to the next size of container.

top 10 permanent plants for shade

- *Adiantum niponicum* 'Pictum' (Japanese painted fern)
- *Clematis alpina* varieties
- *Clematis* hybrids like 'Pink Champagne'
- *Hakonechloa* (Japanese golden grass)
- *Hedera helix* varieties (ivy)
- *Hostas*
- *Pieris*
- *Rhododendron yakushimanum* hybrids
- *Sarcococca* (Christmas box)
- Skimmia varieties

Permanent plants in containers need little care to stay looking good.

Edible pot gardens

Many edible plants grow happily in containers, so even the smallest of gardens can produce luscious strawberries to eat still warm from the sun, tomatoes bursting with flavour and fresh herbs that give the ultimate finishing touch to salads and cooked dishes.

STRAWBERRIES: A SUMMER FEAST

Grow strawberries in high-rise containers to make the maximum use of available space. Tailor-made strawberry pots come in several sizes, from terracotta ones that hold up to a dozen plants, to plastic versions the size of a small dustbin that house up to double that number.

Use a soil-based compost mixed with equal parts by volume of sharp sand or vermiculite (both available from garden centres), and put a layer of drainage material in the base of the pot. It is important to put some sort of channel – for example, a section of drainpipe pierced with holes and surrounded by stones or crocks – in the centre of a large container to ensure that it is watered evenly. The pipe should be the same height as the pot and the top should stand just clear of the soil surface.

Place the container in a sunny, sheltered spot and keep it well watered. Take care not to overfeed the plants. The foliage should be light green – dark green is a sign of too much fertilizer.

STRAWBERRY PLANTS AND VARIETIES

Always buy strawberry plants from a good nursery, garden centre or specialist mail-order supplier. Plant cold-stored runners (young plants) in May or June to be sure of a heavy crop the next summer. Ordinary plants that go in during late summer and early autumn will only give a light crop in their first year. Avoid gifts of plants from other people's gardens as they are very likely to carry virus diseases and will never do well.

Most strawberries crop from mid-June to mid-July, but if you add an early-season variety and a late-season one you pick fruit from early June to late summer. Good varieties for flavour are 'Gorella' and 'Honeyoye' (early); 'Eros' and 'Hapil' (mid); and 'Florence' (late). Perpetual varieties like 'Mara des Bois' produce small amounts of fruit over a long period.

A POTTED HERB GARDEN

Choose herb plants for their looks as well as their culinary uses and you'll have a selection of plants that will look great from spring to autumn at the very least. Evergreen, shrubby types like bay and rosemary look good all year round and add a real touch of class to any garden when clipped into decorative shapes like pyramids or lollipops.

Grow a high-rise feast with a mixture of strawberries and herbs, planted in a tall pot with holes around the sides.

Containers of mixed herbs look attractive but will need regular attention or vigorous plants will mug their slower-growing neighbours. The easiest way to have a handsome potted herb garden is to grow one variety per pot, using containers that are all made from the same material but in different shapes for added interest.

Pot up the plants in soil-based compost with a little extra grit added to ensure good drainage – many herbs hate having wet feet. Most prefer a site in full sun, but parsley and mint are happy in partial shade.

CHOOSING AND CARING FOR HERBS

All herbs come in lots of different varieties and the trick is to pick out the ones with coloured or variegated leaves as these look far more handsome than their green-leaved cousins. Encourage plants to stay neat and produce lots of fresh foliage by trimming them several times a year. Most herbs are perennial so they'll be with you for years; others, such as basil, are annuals and last for one summer only. Parsley can last for a couple of years.

GROWING TOMATOES

If you're really keen you can raise tomatoes from seed sown in late winter, but there's usually no shortage of ready-grown plants on sale in spring.

Time of planting depends on where the tomatoes will be grown. Plant them in February or March in a heated greenhouse, during April in an unheated one and outside in early June. Keep the soil evenly moist

Tomatoes come in all shapes and sizes – even trailing types that can be grown in hanging baskets.

and feed regularly with tomato fertilizer. Bush varieties don't need staking or training but most other types do. Support the main stems with canes or string, and remove sideshoots as they appear. Pinch out the leading shoot when either four trusses (if the plants are growing outside) or six fruit trusses (if they are under cover) have formed.

Below: Pots of herbs look fantastic when placed on a patio and will also smell wonderful on still summer evenings.

top 10 herbs for containers

- *Helichrysum italicum* subsp. *serotinum* (curry plant)
- *Laurus nobilis* (bay)
- *Melissa officinalis* 'Aurea' (lemon balm)
- *Mentha suaveolens* 'Variegata' (pineapple mint)
- *Ocimum basilicum* var. *purpurascens* (purple basil)
- *Origanum vulgare* 'Aureum' (golden marjoram)
- *Petroselinum crispum* (parsley)
- *Rosmarinus officinalis* 'Miss Jessopp's Upright' (rosemary)
- *Salvia officinalis* 'Purpurascens' (purple sage)
- *Thymus* × *citriodorus* 'Silver Queen' (silver lemon thyme)

WATER GARDENING

Water features

Water can transform any garden and can be adapted to suit any site, from a miniature pond or pebble fountain for a tiny garden, to a large pool for a bigger plot. A water feature encourages wildlife, provides a home for plants with unusual and attractive flowers and foliage and, best of all, is tranquil and relaxing – a haven of peace in your garden.

POND CARE

One of the great attractions of water features is that they require very little in the way of maintenance. However, the occasional jobs that need doing are pretty well essential, so make sure nothing gets overlooked. Just how much has to be done depends on what a pond contains. One with a good selection of plants should need hardly any care while one that contains fish will require regular attention. This varies according to the type, size and number of fish – there's little work to be done if you have a couple of goldfish but much more if there are lots of large fish. Lowest of all in the maintenance stakes is a wildlife pond. This type should be pretty much self-sustaining. See pages 112–15 for care of fish and encouraging wildlife.

Several common problems may affect your pond, so do check out this section before leaping into action – or rather the water – as it's all too easy to fall into the 'using a sledgehammer to crack a nut' syndrome. A classic example is cleaning out a pond if the water turns green and then finding out that it wasn't necessary!

GREEN WATER

Green, murky water is caused by microscopic algae which feed on mineral salts or nutrients, and are encouraged to grow by sunlight and warmth. Small or shallow ponds are most susceptible because the water

During winter, keep a hole in the ice of frozen ponds so that oxygen can reach the inhabitants.

can get very warm. If your pond is new, be patient for three seasons – or buy a filter – as your plants will clear the water for you by taking up nutrients and shading the surface.

If an established pond with oxygenating plants and water lilies becomes murky in spring, don't worry. The chances are that the plants will soon be growing vigorously enough to clear the water in a few weeks. If the problem is persistent there could be several possible reasons.

- Topping up pond water from the tap rather than rainwater supplies lots of mineral salts for algae to feed on.
- Overfeeding fish adds surplus nutrients to the pond, again providing food for algae.
- If fertilizers are used nearby they can wash into the pond with similar results.

The problem can usually be solved by the correct balance of planting (see pages 110–11). If the pond contains lots of fish, it may be necessary to fit a large filter to remove their waste (see page 114). Chemical treatments of algae tackle the symptoms, not the cause, so only use one as a last resort.

BLANKET WEED

Blanket weed resembles green cotton wool and is another form of algae with the same causes and solutions as those described above. A quick fix is to pull out the weed by hand or by twirling it round a bamboo cane. Pads made of barley straw or lavender stalks can be sunk in the water and will slow the growth of the weed as they rot down. Use straw ones in small ponds, allowing 20–50g (1–2oz) of straw per square metre. Lavender pads are best suited to larger ponds.

REPAIRING LEAKS

The water level in a pond drops either because of water loss through evaporation in hot weather or because the liner is leaking. If you're unsure of the cause, top up the pond a couple of times and if the level drops quickly and always falls to a certain point you'll know you have a leak. Search for it around the level at which the water stabilizes. You may need to use a stiff brush and clean water to scrub the pond around the water line in order to find the leak.

- Mend fibreglass ponds with a fibreglass car-repair kit.

safety first

Young children can drown in even a few centimetres of water so it is absolutely vital to make water features safe. Safest of all is a moving water feature like a bubble or wall fountain, or one that uses a millstone. A pond can be covered with steel mesh. Lay this just above the surface of the water and paint it black to make it less obvious. A good temporary solution is to lay a piece of stout trellis over the pond.

Make a safe moving water feature without any surface water if there are young children around.

making a pebble fountain

This de luxe pebble fountain is made to a decorative and child-safe design to suit its centre-stage position in a small garden.

1 Mark-out a circle for the feature, which should be no higher in diameter than the intended height of the jet of water from the fountain. Dig a hole for the sump 38cm (15in) deep and wide. Put down a layer of sand on which to place the liner, which should stretch right up to the paving. A cheap PVC liner can be used for this type of feature as it won't be exposed to sunlight that would cause the material to degrade. Put the pump in the pond, with the cable running through a piece of plastic pipe, then put down a layer of mortar. Using a builders' trowel, take out some of the mortar around the rim to create a sunken 'collar' about 2.5cm (1in) deep and 7.5cm (3in) wide.

2 Starting at the outside edge, place the pebbles closely in a circle, then work inwards and repeat. Tap the pebbles gently into the mortar using a piece of wood to ensure the stones are level.

3 Steel rods are set into the cement in a criss-cross pattern to ensure this feature is utterly child-safe. Kneeling on a plank spreads your weight on the newly laid pebbles.

4 Steel mesh is cut to fit the opening, then tied to the rods with wire. Fill the sump with water, then hide the mesh with cobbles. Trim the liner to fit closely up to the paving. Hide the edges with pebbles set in cement.

5 Turn on the pump and adjust the height of the jet. During winter, run the pump for a few minutes every couple of weeks. In an exposed garden, the pump should be taken out and stored for the winter.

- Butyl liners can be repaired easily with sticky patches of special material, similar to those used to mend a bicycle puncture. Bale out more water so that the level is well below that of the leak – you won't need to remove fish and plants provided about 15cm (6in) of water remains in the pond. Leave the liner to dry for about 24 hours, then clean all around the hole. Cut a patch that allows a good overlap all round and stick it on, following the manufacturer's instructions. Check that the patch is firmly bonded after about 24 hours and, if it is, refill the pond.
- If a concrete liner has one or two leaks near the top – generally the result of deep cracks – it can be repaired fairly easily. Lower the water level as above and leave the liner to dry out. Clean the area around each crack, then chisel out the crack so that it's at least 3cm (1in) deeper than the original break and chip the surface of the surrounding area to roughen it. Fill the crack with waterproof mastic cement and leave to dry, following the manufacturer's instructions. Finally, treat the area with a sealing compound. If a pond has a number of leaks or is cracking with age, reline it with a flexible liner.
- Cheap PVC liners can't be mended and the only solution is to fit a new one.

DOING A MAJOR POND CLEAN-OUT

A pond needs to be cleaned out every five to seven years when the sediment at the bottom has reached a depth of 15–18cm (6–7in). Late spring is the time to do this, so that the pond can settle down before winter.

Take out the plants and divide and repot them if necessary, then, if the water is polluted, drain it all out. Bale or siphon out some of the water leaving a good amount (and the fish) in the pond. Use a fine net to scoop out the sediment from the base of the pond, but don't worry about taking out every last bit. Pile the sediment on a polythene sheet next to the pond and leave it there for a couple of days so that any creatures can make their way back to the water.

Replace the plants and top up the water level – with rainwater if at all possible.

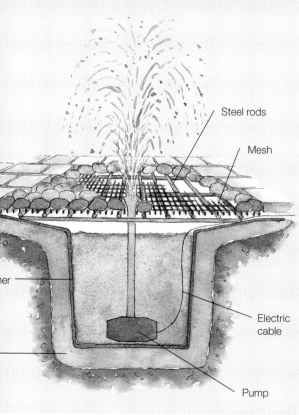

Steel rods

Mesh

ner

Electric cable

Pump

Maintaining water features

The range of water features is enormous, but basically they break down into two categories: conventional ponds, either sunken or raised – small container ponds are just about the simplest to care for – or features like fountains and waterfalls that involve moving water and rather more work to install. The pebble fountain in this chapter is about as low maintenance as you can get.

CONTAINER PONDS

Almost any container can be used to make a pond, but small ones produce specific problems. Because there is little water, it's subject to wide variations in temperature and there are likely to be problems with algae in summer. Provided a small pond has space for a couple of pond plants these will help to combat

algae, but a feature that is designed to hold only water – a stone bowl, for example – is best treated with a chemical known as an algicide.

Certain types of container are only suitable for use from spring to autumn, while others can remain outdoors all year. The water in small raised ones is liable to freeze solid in winter. Any fish, plants or wildlife will be killed and the container itself may break. Either move the entire pond under cover for the winter, or empty the container and store it. If it's too heavy to be moved, drain it and, if possible, turn it upside down to keep rainwater out. Keep fish and water plants in bowls of water in a cold but frost-free porch, greenhouse or conservatory.

Larger containers like wooden half-barrels can stay outside in a sheltered spot. However, it's worth removing any living creatures and choice pond plants such as water lilies in case the weather turns very cold.

PUMPS

A fountain or waterfall is powered by a pump and as this is a relatively expensive piece of equipment it deserves regular tender loving care. Site it in the lowest part of the pond or water reservoir, but sit it on a brick so that it doesn't draw in the sediment that builds up on the floor of the pond, and which will clog it up. The filter collects the sediment and must be taken out and rinsed in clean water every couple of weeks – more often if the water is murky, or if the flow starts slowing down. It's worth fitting a pre-filter if the pump clogs up frequently. Always switch off and unplug the pump before doing any maintenance. Clean fountain nozzles regularly as they may become blocked. If the jets clog up, poke the dirt out of the holes using a straightened paperclip, or pull off the fountain head and clean it under running water.

A half-barrel makes a perfect miniature pond. However, it's not ideal for fish as water becomes hot in summer and freezes in winter.

warning

Water and electricity are a potentially fatal combination. If you're running a pump off the mains supply, always use a circuit breaker so that the electricity is cut off if a fault occurs. Where possible, use a low-voltage pump. All fittings and cables must be designed for outdoor use, and should be checked at least once a year for any signs of wear.

Left: Follow instructions when installing a pump, and always use equipment that is designed for outdoor use. *Below*: A moving water feature with a covered reservoir of water needs very little care.

building a rill

Built with railway-sleeper sides and a slate bottom, this rill makes an enchanting centrepiece to a garden. However, even the *Ground Force* team found it tricky going, so this is something for the experienced DIY person to tackle. This feature needs more water than the reservoir contains, so before the pump was switched on, the channel was filled from the top with a hose.

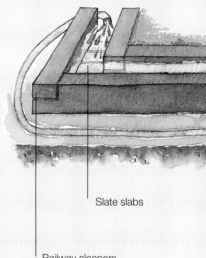

Slate slabs

Railway sleepers, screwed together

2 The railway sleepers need to fit at right angles to each other, so a chunk is chainsawed out of the end of each one to make a neat joint and the sleepers are then screwed together.

1 Digging out the channels with the correct drop is all-important to create a gentle yet continuous trickle of water. The level drops no more than 30cm (12in) from one end of this large feature to the other – a drop of around 5cm (2in) for each straight section. Put a thick bed of sand on the base of the channel and tamp it down firmly with a piece of timber. Then, line the whole of the channel with butyl liner. As the feature measures around 14m (46ft) from beginning to end, this meant sticking sections of liner together with special adhesive.

3 Cut the slate to fit the base of the channel. The best way of doing this is to half-bury a garden spade in the ground to form a firm edge on which to rest the slate, then chop off the protruding bit of slate using a builders' trowel.

4 The water reservoir consists of a plastic water butt buried in the ground at the lower end, and contains the submersible pump. A piece of 1¼ internal bore pipe circulates the water up to the top of the rill.

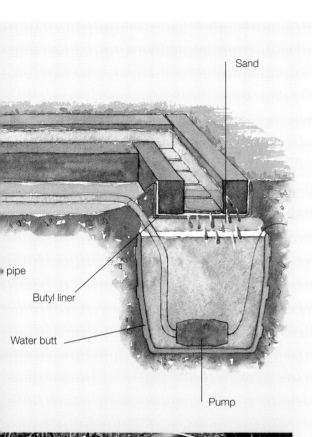

Sand

pipe

Butyl liner

Water butt

Pump

WINTER CARE FOR PUMPS

A pump that isn't used during winter should be taken out, cleaned thoroughly in fresh water, dried and stored according to the manufacturer's instructions. A pond heater could take its place and will keep a small area of water ice-free. If the pump remains in place over winter it must be covered by at least 45cm (18in) of water to prevent it freezing. Once a fortnight run it for a short time to prevent sediment building up.

PEBBLE FOUNTAINS

The pump in a pebble fountain needs the kind of care described above, except that the filter can be cleaned far less frequently because the reservoir of water is covered and, consequently, there shouldn't be too much sediment.

Keep the water level topped up. It's hard to remember to do this because the reservoir is hidden from sight, but regular topping up is very important during hot weather when the water evaporates quickly. Also bear in mind that when the weather is windy, a tall fountain jet may fall outside the edge of the water reservoir. You'll either need to lower the jet, or remember to top up the water level more often. In spring, give the pebbles a good scrub if they are looking a bit green and grubby. If you're adding new ones, rinse them first to remove any dust or lime that could contaminate the water. Bearing in mind the amount of maintenance you'll need to do, think carefully about positioning your water feature so that you'll have relatively easy access.

REPAIRING A WATERFALL

If the level of the water in a pond beneath a waterfall drops, check to see whether it's the pond or the waterfall that's leaking. Switch off the waterfall for a couple of days, top up the pond and see if the water level drops. Then switch the waterfall on again to see if it is the culprit.

Finding the leak can be tricky. Your best bet is to wait for a spell of dry weather and then look for a telltale damp patch of soil. Failing that, line the entire waterfall area with flexible liner.

Plants for ponds

A well-planted pond is not only likely to be clear and healthy but, with the right selection of plants, it should look terrific from spring to autumn. Water plants aren't subject to summer droughts, so they will be lush and green even when the rest of the garden is fainting in the heat.

MARGINALS

These plants live in shallow water around the pond's edge or margin, hence their name. They soften its hard outlines and help it to blend in with the rest of the garden. They also provide valuable shelter for all sorts of wildlife.

Every spring, feed the plants with tablets or sachets of a slow-release fertilizer that's designed for use in ponds. Never use ordinary plant fertilizer as this will cause appalling problems with green water. When plant growth has died back naturally in autumn it should be cut back to just above water level. Avoid going below the water line as some varieties have hollow stems and could be killed.

Once marginals are over five years old, they tend to form large, overcrowded clumps and their performance starts to go downhill. They can be rejuvenated by division, in exactly the same way as for herbaceous perennials (see page 74).

WATER LILIES

Water lilies are the aristocrats of the pond, but unfortunately we pay for this beauty in that they can suffer from several pests and diseases. It's worth it, though, to see those spectacular blooms. They play an important role in keeping a pond healthy as their large leaves keep sunlight off the water, helping to stop the growth of green algae.

They vary enormously in vigour from dwarf varieties suitable for a container pond, to fast-growing ones that need a small lake, so it is important to choose wisely. If the leaves are being pushed right out of the water, the variety of water lily is too vigorous for your size of pond.

A plant can produce so many leaves in summer that they become overcrowded, so thin out the leaves with secateurs. Start by removing any that are starting to turn yellow. Once the leaves have yellowed and died back in autumn, cut them off and remove them or they will rot down and pollute the pond.

Any plants that have become large and overcrowded can be divided after six or seven years. In spring, lift the plant out and wash off the soil so you can see its roots. Use a sharp knife to cut off the smaller rootstocks or sideshoots where they join the main stem. Replant the sideshoots and throw out the old rootstock.

Miniature water lilies are suitable for tiny ponds such as barrels. They prefer to be planted in about 15–30cm (6–12in) of water. *Nymphaea pygmaea* 'Helvola' bears soft yellow flowers, *Nymphaea pygmaea* 'Alba' is white and *Nymphaea pygmaea* 'Rubra' opens rose-pink and

Small water lilies like *N*. 'Froebeli' tend to cost more than larger varieties, but are perfect for a small pond.

marginal plants for ponds

There is a wide selection of plants that can be grown around the edges of a pond. Water-loving irises make a magnificent summer display – this variety is *Iris laevigata* 'Colchesterensis'.

The upright foliage of grass-like plants makes a handsome contrast to bushy plants. *Butomus umbellatus* (flowering rush) has attractive leaves and produces pretty rose-pink flowers in summer.

The kingcup or marsh marigold (*Caltha palustris*) is one of the first marginal plants to bloom in spring, making a wonderful display of golden flowers.

ages to red. *Nymphaea* 'Laydekeri' varieties are pale pink, rose-pink or rosy-crimson in colour.

Small water lilies are ideal for a pond measuring 1.2–1.5m (4–5ft) and should be planted in water 30–45cm (12–18in) deep. *Nymphaea* 'Aurora' opens yellow and ages to orange then red. *Nymphaea* 'Froebeli' is deep blood-red. *Nymphaea* 'James Brydon' has carmine-red flowers. *Nymphaea* 'Hermine' is pure white. *Nymphaa* 'Laydekeri' varieties (see above) are also suitable for this size of pond.

Medium water lilies are suitable for ponds measuring at least 1.8–2.4m (6–8ft) and should be planted in 45–75cm (18–30in) of water. *Nymphaea* 'Conqueror' is bright red flecked with white. *Nymphaea* 'Gonnere' (also known as 'Snowball') has double, pure-white flowers. *Nymphaea Marliacea* 'Albida' is pure white. *Nymphaea Marliacea* 'Chromatella' has soft primrose-yellow flowers. *Nymphaea* William B. Shaw' is pale shell-pink.

Large water lilies are very vigorous and should only be grown in pools measuring 3m (10ft) and above, and with

water that is at least 60cm (24in) deep. *Nymphaea alba* is pure white. *Nymphaea* 'Attraction' is deep red. *Nymphaea* 'Escarboucle' has dark crimson flowers. *Nymphaea Marliacea* 'Carnea' is pale pink with a deeper tint right at the base of the petals.

Pests to watch out for are water lily aphids which make the leaves look unsightly, and water lily beetles which eat the leaves. The beetles come in two forms: brown adults about 1cm (½ in) long and black grubs. Aphids are reasonably rare and the best way to control them is to pick as many as you can off the leaves, then wash off the remainder with a hose for fish to eat. The best way to deal with the beetles is to weigh the leaves down under the water so that pond creatures can feast on them. Don't use chemicals as they will kill fish and wildlife.

Water lily leaf spot can be a problem during spells of damp, warm weather. The spots appear on the leaves and eventually rot with the result that holes develop. Control by picking off the affected leaves.

Pontederia cordata (pickerel weed) is a beautiful marginal plant for late summer colour, producing dense spikes of soft blue flowers above glossy, heart-shaped leaves.

OXYGENATORS

Oxygenators live in the deepest water and are the hard-working backroom boys of pond life. They play an important role in keeping a pond healthy by taking up waste products given off by fish and other creatures, and absorbing mineral salts that would otherwise provide food for green algae. Oxygenators are sold in bunches which are best planted in net pots (see opposite).

The plants can be growing at quite a rate by mid-summer and will need thinning from time to time. It's best to cut them back little and often rather than having one great blitz. If any plants are out of reach, use a rake to pull out foliage – but take care not to puncture the lining of the pond. Pile foliage cut from the plants, and sediment dredged from the bottom, by the

edge of the pond for a couple of days to allow any pond creatures to make their way back to the water.

FLOATING PLANTS

Floating aquatic plants drift on the water's surface with their roots dangling free. They play a practical role by shading the water from too much sunlight and look pretty into the bargain. Some varieties like frogbit and water soldier are hardy and can stay in the pond all year. Others – water hyacinth and water lettuce, for example – are frost-tender and must be overwintered in a bowl of water in a light frost-free place like the window sill of a cool room.

Although floaters rarely grow to such an extent that they need thinning out, this may happen in a very warm summer. Simply scoop out surplus plants if necessary.

Beware of thugs

Several thuggish plants have escaped from garden ponds and are starting to cause serious problems in our waterways. These are: *Myriophyllum aquaticum* (parrot's feather); *Crassula helmsii*, also sold as *Tillaea recurva* or *T. helmsii* (Australian swamp stonecrop); *Hydrocotyle ranunculoides* (floating pennywort); and *Azolla filiculoides* and *A. caroliniana* (water fern or fairy fern).

If you have any of these plants, pull them out of your pond and burn, bury or compost them to reduce the risk of their spreading to the wild.

HOW TO PLANT A POND

Water plants are essential in order to have a clear, healthy pond that needs the minimum of maintenance. Choosing the correct combination of plants will ensure that your pond is a healthy, balanced environment for fish and other creatures, and the water will be naturally clear. This means less work for you, which has to be good news. A pond without plants is open to sunlight, which encourages the rapid growth of green algae. Although not harmful, a pond filled with green water isn't very attractive, and it's frustrating when you know the water contains fish and other creatures that can't be seen.

Plant up the pond any time from mid-spring to late summer. Start with the deep-water plants, primarily water lillies which have large, rounded leaves that are great for shading the water. Choose water lilies of a suitable size to match your pond and plant these in containers (see box, below). Water lilies and other deep-water pond plants need to be gradually acclimatized to their final depth. To do this, either stand the container in the pond on a small stack of bricks and remove them gradually over a couple of weeks, or suspend the container on strings attached to the ground on opposite sides of the pond. Then, plant oxygenating plants that also need to go in deep water – one for every 0.09sq m (1sq ft). Eventually, aim to cover about a third to a half of the water's surface with shade-creating foliage.

Now plant the marginal plants that will sit on planting shelves around the pond edges. Eventually the marginals should take up between a third to a half of the perimeter of the pond. Finally, launch any floating plants onto the surface of the water.

Among the ornamental plants that can be grown in deep water is *Orontium aquaticum* (golden club), which produces its unusually shaped flowers in late spring.

preparing an aquatic plant for a pond

1 Aquatic plants are best planted in containers that have mesh sides. Those made of large mesh will need lining first. Plant using special compost for aquatic plants – not ordinary potting compost.

2 Leave a gap of about 1cm (½in) between the compost and the rim of the pot. Finish off with a layer of fine gravel that will stop the soil floating away.

3 Water the container thoroughly using a watering can fitted with a fine rose, then place the plant in the pond. Plants that are going in deep water need to be lowered down gradually over a couple of weeks.

Fish

Fish bring a lively and colourful touch to a pond and many people find watching their antics relaxing and enjoyable. To be sure of healthy, long-lived specimens, it is important to choose the type and quantity that suit your pond and to create a healthy environment for them all year round.

THE RIGHT KIND OF POND

Check out your pond before buying any fish. If you want the fish to be year-round inhabitants you need a pond that is at least 60cm (2ft) deep at one point so that the water doesn't overheat in summer or freeze in winter. A smaller pond can house fish for part of the year, but take care to avoid the sunniest spots where they may get too hot in warm weather. They will have to be moved to a frost-free tank indoors over winter.

A fountain or waterfall looks eye-catching in any pond, and will also help to keep your fish happy. In summer the splashing water will introduce life-giving oxygen to the pond when it tends to become low in hot weather, and in winter the pump can be replaced with a pond heater. If you want large numbers of fish or Koi carp, you will need a filter of some sort (see page 114).

WHICH FISH?

Small ponds are best suited to goldfish – the easiest fish of all – plus Shubunkins and Comets. As a guide to how many fish your pond will be able to take, allow

A water feature can look stylish, yet also make provision for wildlife. The gravel 'beach' provides access for birds and other creatures to drink and bathe with ease.

2.5cm (1in) of fish to every 0.09 sq m (1sq ft) of water surface. Golden Orfe require a larger pond with a minimum surface area of at least 4.6 sq m (50 sq ft). These colourful and active fish are sociable and should be introduced in groups of at least four. Koi carp are only for real enthusiasts. These expensive, fast-growing fish need a large pond – 2.5 sq m (3 sq yd) for each carp – which must be fitted with a filtration system as they will uproot and kill any water plants. They also require protection from sunburn in summer and a heater in winter.

PUTTING FISH IN A POND

Before you put fish in your pond you need to make sure it is well-planted (see pages 110–11) as the water should be clear and healthy, and free of excessive oxygen-absorbing algae. Plant foliage provides shelter from the sun and predators and a home for natural fish food like tiny insects; and it is also a place for egg-laying should your fish feel inclined to breed.

Plant up a pond several weeks before introducing the fish so that the plants have time to establish. Float the bag of fish in the pond for about half an hour so that the temperature of the water inside it stabilizes to that of the pond. Open the bag to let some pond water in and allow the fish to swim out a few minutes later.

FEEDING FISH

Small numbers of fish can survive by feeding on the natural food provided by the plants in a pond, but if you have lots of fish, or large specimens, they will need special food in the form of flakes (for small fish) and pellets or sticks (for larger ones).

Feed fish once a day, starting with small amounts in spring as the temperature rises, and decreasing in autumn with the arrival of cooler weather. If you feed them regularly at the same time and place they will soon cluster there in anticipation. They won't need feeding at all in winter as they live off the reserves in their bodies. Only give as much food as will be eaten within ten minutes. Overfeeding is a common cause of green water because anything that is uneaten adds nutrients and encourages algae to thrive.

Place new fish in a bag of water and float them on your pond for half an hour before releasing them.

CARING FOR FISH IN WINTER

Freezing weather spells danger to fish and any other creatures within the pond, like frogs and toads that hibernate in the sediment on the pond floor. Once a solid layer of ice has built up on the surface of the pond toxic gases build up underneath and there is no way that oxygen can get in.

Just a small area of the pond needs to be kept free of ice. If you have a pond pump that is powered by electricity you can use this for a little pond heater that will keep a patch of water clear of ice. Alternatively, float several large balls in the pond and, when the water freezes, remove one to leave a clear patch. It's important to use more than one ball, which might freeze over if the day stays very cold.

Never break ice by hitting it. The shock waves could concuss and kill the creatures in the pond. Instead, melt a hole by standing a saucepan filled with boiling water on the ice.

Water and wildlife

Water is essential for survival, so it's not surprising that all sorts of creatures are irresistibly drawn to ponds. Birds visit them to drink and bathe; frogs, toads and newts breed in the water and spend a good part of their time in it; and dragonflies, the most spectacular of insects, perform dramatic aerial displays. A pond will soon teem with all manner of fascinating life, from tiny pond-dwelling insects to birds.

All this wildlife has spin-off benefits for the gardener, as many of the creatures that are attracted to a pond also feed on garden pests. However, it is worth mentioning that fish and wildlife don't really go hand-in-hand as fish eat tadpoles and many other small creatures.

Wait for wildlife to arrive in your pond of its own accord, unless a nearby pond has stacks of frog- and toadspawn in spring. Taking spawn from ponds that are some way off could encourage the spread of disease.

MAKING A POND WILDLIFE-FRIENDLY

Ideally, a pond should be built with wildlife in mind, but if this isn't the case with yours it's not too difficult to alter it so that it provides maximum value and minimum danger for all kinds of creatures.

Steep, shelving sides all around a pond can be a deathtrap to animals like hedgehogs that come to drink and end up drowning. Even frogs and toads can drown if they can't get out of the water. If you make one side into a gently shelving pebble or cobble 'beach' you'll be rewarded by lots of birds perching to drink and bathe. If this isn't possible, put piles of cobbles in the corners of the pond for easy access.

A paved border that completely surrounds a pond is offputting to wildlife – and baby frogs and toads can actually fry trying to cross sunbaked slabs. Make a 'green corridor' by planting marginal and ground-cover plants so that they spread across parts of the paving.

For an ultra-good wildlife pond, include some species that directly benefit certain creatures in your choice of pond plants. Bees and butterflies feed on the flowers of plants like *Caltha palustris* (kingcup), *Mentha aquatica* (water mint), *Myosotis scorpioides* (water forget-me-not) and *Lythrum salicaria* (purple loosestrife). Dragonflies and damselflies breed on plants like grasses, rushes and irises that have vertical stems. Remember, too, that the more plants you have the more cover there is for wildlife.

FILTERS AND UV CLARIFIERS

If you have lots of fish, add a filter to the pump to remove their waste products and keep the water clear. This applies particularly if there are only a few plants in your pond. Mechanical filters work like fine sieves to remove tiny particles and green algae. Biological filters are more expensive and more complex, but extremely effective. For crystal-clear water, add an ultraviolet (UV) clarifier to the system.

HERONS: THE NO. 1 ENEMY

Most birds are welcome visitors but fish-owners tend to get very hot under the collar about herons – hardly surprising as just one adult bird can eat as many as ten small goldfish in a day. They also eat other creatures like frogs.

Stretching a net about 30cm (12in) above the pond makes for effective protection but looks more than a bit ugly. It's much less intrusive to run a strong fishing line or stout string around the pond and stretch it taut at a height of about 30cm (12in), and 60cm (24in) back from the edge of the pond. This usually works because herons land a short way from a pond and step towards the water's edge to fish. Failing that, it would be worth buying a bird-scarer that triggers something like a loud noise or a visual deterrent.

Opposite: **The water in a newly built feature is cloudy, but will soon clear and the sloping sides of this stream give good access for wildlife.**

how to plant a wildlife pond

While all ponds attract wildlife to some degree, a pond that is planned for that purpose will encourage all sorts of creatures to visit your garden and even take up residence there. A wildlife pond is easy to build and maintain too.

Easy access to the water is vital, so at least one side should be gently shelving and made with a pebble and gravel 'beach'. For a natural appearance, hide the edge of the liner all around the pond with smooth stones and plants – both marginal plants within the pond and garden plants in the surrounding soil that will tumble over the edge.

The pond plants can either go in submerged containers as described on page 111, or a layer of garden soil can be placed in the base of the pond and the plants can go into the muddy bottom.

Plants for a wildlife pond should either be native ones or should have some benefit to wildlife.

Site marginal plants in the shallow water around the pond edge

Site water lilies and deep-water aquatics in the deepest part of the pond

Oxygenating plants also like deep water

GARDEN FEATURES

Decorative structures

ARCHES

All upright structures make a huge difference to a garden and an arch is the easiest to construct. There are loads of different designs and materials, the choice of which depends on your DIY abilities and, of course, your budget. Money aside, the main decision is whether to buy a ready-made arch in kit form, or whether you're feeling ambitious enough to make your own using sawn timber.

Like most things, arches definitely fall into the 'you get what you pay for' bracket. The cheapest ready-made ones are made of plastic-covered metal or flimsy trellis, but won't last very long. Stronger arches made of timber, stout trellis, nylon-coated steel tubing or wrought iron are a much better bet as they'll last for many years and be strong enough to support a decent amount of plant growth. Woven willow or hazel arches look a real treat in a country-style garden and will last

for a reasonable length of time. Whatever type of arch you opt for, always make sure it's put up with a sound footing (see page 129) as it's likely to become top-heavy when the plants grow.

Arches can be sited in lots of places around the garden. One over a front gate emphasizes the feeling of coming home, particularly if you train some nicely scented plants over it. Similarly, put an archway between two different areas in the garden to highlight the difference between them. If you have a long pathway, use a series of several arches to create a plant-clad 'tunnel'. An arch can also be used to create a quick, easy and effective little arbour. Site it against a fence, hedge or trellis and simply put a seat underneath.

Arches come in all sorts of materials. This woven willow and hazel arch would look perfect in a country setting.

ARBOURS

Arbours, gazebos and summerhouses are all for sitting in, but an arbour is open to the weather while a gazebo has a solid roof and open sides and a summerhouse is completely solid. Because an arbour uses fewer materials than either of the other buildings, it's the cheapest way of making an attractive and sheltered spot away from the house. Ideally, site it so that it provides a focal point in the garden's design, and gets the sun at a different time to the patio or main seating area. Train climbing plants over the framework to create shade and shelter as well as colour and scent.

For a small, simple arbour, place an arch large enough to house a bench against a wall, fence or hedge, or enclose it with trellis. A number of ready-made arbours that follow this basic design are available, but vary enormously in style and materials with prices to match – from three to four figures.

Larger arbours measuring around 2.4m (8ft) square are more sheltered and secluded. Again there are many ready-made models, or make your own using 100mm (4in) square posts, with 50×100mm (2×4in) timber for the framework and beams.

Where space is limited, a good compromise between the designs described above is a triangular arbour which can be tucked into all but the smallest corner of the garden. Make it with three corner posts and with the overhead beams running diagonally.

PERGOLAS

A pergola is an open structure made of timber, with a framework of posts supporting rafters set fairly close together, over which climbing plants can scramble. If your patio is uncomfortably sunbaked, copy our continental neighbours and build a pergola to transform it into an area of lovely dappled shade that is absolutely perfect for eating and relaxing. Another good place for a pergola is over a pathway where a long, slender structure brings height to a garden, as well as making a transition from one area to another.

A patio next to the house is ideal for a lean-to pergola. The 150×50mm (6×2in) rafters are supported on the house side by a beam attached to the wall, and on the

Make a simple arbour by putting a ready-made arch against a fence with a bench placed underneath.

other by several 100×100mm (4×4in) upright posts. If there is no supporting wall available, the whole structure can be freestanding and supported by posts. Pergolas are available in kit form, but to get one to fit the site in your garden it may be necessary to build your own. It's worth roping in a couple of volunteers to help with lifting the beams into place so that you can get on with checking levels, drilling and fixing everything securely.

Plant growth on pergolas will become dense in time and as it will not only be heavy in its own right, but will also catch any strong winds, the pergola needs to be on a very secure footing. Each upright should be bedded in post holes to a depth of at least 30cm (1ft) in a sound footing of ballast and cement (see page 129). In the early years climbing plants will need some help to scramble up the posts. Either train the stems upwards using wire, or surround each post with fine wire mesh.

Care and maintenance

All wooden structures should be treated with preservative every couple of years (see page 133). A bit of regular maintenance will definitely pay off in the long term. Pay particular attention to the points where the structure enters the soil as it is a major job to replace posts on arches, arbours or pergolas. For this reason,when choosing plants to train onto a pergola, it's a good idea to choose climbing plants that are either pruned regularly, such as rambler roses and clematis, or ones like passion flower and golden hop that don't mind being hacked back.

TRELLIS

What would we do in the garden without trellis! It can be adapted to a host of uses: fixed on to walls and fences as a support for climbing plants; as a screen to divide the garden, shield the patio or hide anything

A pergola and other large vertical features need to be put up very securely, particularly if they will be supporting a lot of plant growth.

don't scrimp on size

It may sound blindingly obvious, but be sure to buy or make an arch or arbour that is both high enough (at least 2m/6½ft) and wide enough. Remember that plant growth will spread out – and down – for quite a way and there must be enough room to pass through the structure easily. This applies particularly to arches over paths.

In a tiny garden think vertical. A rustic arbour provides a tempting place in which to sit, the hazel hurdles make an attractive screen and a wigwam of poles creates height in the border.

When constructing a trellis screen, consider using trellis with a wavy top or with a 'window' in the middle.

ugly; in containers as freestanding supports for climbers; and on the tops of fences and walls to extend them and create extra privacy without claustrophobia.

Trellis comes in panels of many shapes, sizes and designs, so take a good look at what's available before you buy. The more decorative types are obviously more expensive, but they contain much more wood than the cheapest ones and therefore last longer. If you only want trellis as a support for plants on a wall or fence, opt for the simplest and cheapest squared type as the plants will eventually cover it completely. A freestanding screen will be much more visible and it's worth going for a more attractive design, maybe with a wave-topped finish. Add a stylish touch by topping each post with a decorative finial (post cap) in the shape of an acorn or something similar.

Care and maintenance

Trellis should be thoroughly treated with wood stain or preservative before it goes up, and treated again every couple of years. Access to trellis in future years could be a problem once it becomes covered with plant growth.

Where it is important to keep the trellis looking good, such as with a high-profile trellis screen, or where you can see it directly from your living room, choose climbing plants that are herbaceous in habit – that is, they die back to ground level every autumn – or those that will put up with being hard pruned. Good candidates include *Clematis viticella* varieties, *Eccremocarpus scaber* (Chilean glory flower), *Humulus lupulus* 'Aureus' (golden hop), *Lathyrus latifolius* (perennial pea), and *Passiflora caerulea* (passion flower). Alternatively, you can train wall shrubs on one side of the trellis only, so that they can be untied and laid carefully on the ground while you carry out all necessary maintenance.

Garden accessories

BARBECUES

If you enjoy eating outside, a barbecue is an essential. There are stacks of different portable ones from small basic models to massive grills complete with more gadgets than you could imagine using. Gas-powered models are also available and make the barbecuing process quicker, cleaner and easier – but there is the downside of lugging a heavy gas bottle about.

Keen BBQ chefs often fancy permanent barbecues, but it's worth thinking long and hard before starting to build one as it will take pole position on the patio and look a lot less than beautiful. Even a cheap, cheerful and movable model made out of an old oil drum needs

A chiminea beats a barbecue for looks and can stay out on the patio to make an attractive and unusual feature.

permanent brick pillars. Whatever the type of barbecue, make sure the grill is large enough, then buy one size bigger than you think you'll need. Most importantly, it must be easy to remove the grill for cleaning.

Siting a barbecue

Whether a barbecue is movable or a permanent fixture, it needs to be at the centre of the action – convenient for both the kitchen and the outdoor eating area. The cook will be standing over it for a fair amount of time and won't want to be miles away from his or her guests. Choose a favoured spot that is sheltered from the wind, away from potential fire hazards like fences and not so close to windows that smoke billows indoors. Some outdoor lighting is handy, and a few herbs nearby are great for picking and chucking on to the barbecue for that last-minute finishing touch.

FURNITURE

Garden furniture comes in an enormous variety of styles, designs and materials – not to mention prices that range from cheap to astronomical. First decide on a budget and then work out how many items of furniture you need to buy. Most people go for a table and four chairs, plus a couple of extra seats for visitors, and usually a parasol plus base for a bit of shade. Garden loungers or steamer chairs are great if you want to really stretch out and relax. However, bear in mind that everything will have to be stored somewhere so check the available space in your shed or garage. Depending on the layout of your garden, you may also want a traditional garden bench which will provide somewhere permanent to sit. This can form an important design feature by creating a focal point within the garden.

Garden centres and DIY stores usually offer a decent range of furniture. You can also use mail-order companies – but it's often best to try before you buy. A big garden show in your area is great news as masses of different furniture will be on sale, allowing you to compare all types and prices with ease. If you're planning to buy anything made of hardwood, check the origins of the timber in case it is from a country where illegal logging is commonplace. If at all possible, try to buy timber that is approved by the Forestry Stewardship Council.

Care and maintenance

Furniture should be put away for the winter, or protected under tailor-made plastic covers if you don't have enough space. Wooden furniture that is stored indoors should be treated with a suitable wood stain or oil every year or two. Treat benches or other pieces that are outside year-round every autumn.

Right: A garden seat doesn't have to be a traditional bench – make your own individual design using a piece of driftwood on log supports.

Below: Tailor-make your furniture to fit your plot. This tree seat is made in two halves that are then fitted together.

Surface selection

DECKING

Decking, or wooden flooring for outdoors, is a *Ground Force* favourite. Wood is warm underfoot, dries out quickly because water runs through it, and looks good almost anywhere in the garden.

Decking has more than a few advantages over paving, the chief one being that you are a lot less limited by the layout of your garden. Areas that would be a nuisance or downright impossible to pave, like sloping sites or around existing trees, can accommodate a deck and you won't need to slave over a massive soil-moving job. Unlike patios, decks can be built to a whisker below the damp-proof course, so there's no need to have awkward steps

right next to the house. And because decking is lighter than paving, it is ideal for awkward spots like roof gardens or split-level houses that need a high-level deck – in effect, one that is built on stilts. However, constructing a high-level deck is a job that is best left to professionals unless you're very good at building.

The success of a deck depends on a good foundation. All decks are built on a framework of joists. These are usually made of 150 × 50mm (6 × 2in) timber and should be spaced no more than 40cm (16in) apart. Each of the joists must be supported from below at less than 3m (10ft) intervals. If the supports are further apart, the dimensions of the timber for the joists increase to 200 × 50mm (8 × 2in). The decking boards are laid at right angles on top of the framework of joists. If you want to lay them in patterns or at contrasting angles, the joists must be constructed so that the boards still go at right angles.

The timber for making a DIY deck is usually European redwood or spruce. Always buy timber that has been pressure-treated with preservative, and remember to treat any newly sawn surfaces with more of the same to stop the damp getting in. Professional decking firms offer a wider choice of wood. Tropical hardwood costs a packet and is really tough, but make sure it is certified by the Forest Stewardship Council. Southern yellow pine and western red cedar are also very good but almost as pricey.

Decking-board finishes

Boards come in plain or ribbed finishes. Some people prefer the first because it's less slippery when wet, but others find it uncomfortable. Walk on a few samples before you buy. Beware laying ribbed decking in patterns – it looks great to begin with but is a nightmare to keep clean.

Decking can be constructed to whatever shape fits your garden best. A ribbed finish is less slippery when wet.

The boards can be stained different colours, but use a special, hard-wearing decking stain rather than a general-purpose wood stain. All new decking can be treated with a sealant that helps keep out the damp and reduces the growth of mould and algae.

Care and maintenance

If possible, site a deck in a sunny spot so it dries out quickly after rain. The most important maintenance job is sweeping the deck regularly with a stiff brush to keep it clean. Once or twice a year, use a proprietary decking cleaner. Ribbed surfaces may need blasting with a high-powered pressure-washer to remove all the dirt. Once the wood is clean and dry it can be treated with decking oil to replace some natural oils that have been lost.

A large patio that forms the centrepiece of a garden needs to be planned and built with care.

PAVING

Large paved areas like patios and paths are the bones of your garden and will stare you in the face throughout the year, so it's vital to plan their size and layout and to build them properly. Well-laid paving will last for many years, so put down the best materials you can afford. Take your time and do the job properly as the work that goes into the bits that are out-of-sight will directly affect the good looks of the paving.

All paving must be based on a firm foundation, the thickness and type of which depends on the amount of weight the paving is likely to carry. Lay a patio or path on a mortar mix about 10cm (4in) thick, made up of 4 parts sharp sand, 2 parts soft sand and 1 part cement, mixed with enough water to make it soft but not runny. However, a driveway for cars needs a hardcore and concrete base at least 15cm (6in) thick with the mortar on top of this and the slabs laid on the mortar.

Gravel makes a versatile and inexpensive hard surface for a low-maintenance garden.

When laying paving next to a house, it's vital to leave a gap of about 15cm (6in) between it and the damp-proof course. Slope the paving so that it falls away from the house – about 1cm in every metre (⅜in in every yard). This will prevent rainwater building up against the walls.

Paving slabs come in a wide range of sizes, styles and colours, both in natural stone and man-made alternatives. Natural stone looks wonderful but is expensive, and some of the imitations look almost as good. The simplest paving design is made with slabs that are all the same size, or several different sizes can be combined for a 'random' effect. Make sure your chosen paving looks good with your house – it's worth buying a sample slab before you commit to a firm order.

Care and maintenance

Properly laid paving needs very little maintenance apart from a regular sweeping to prevent a build-up of moss and algae. In winter, use a pressure-washer or proprietary cleaner on the slabs as damp, dirty ones can become dangerously slippery.

GRAVEL

A lot of *Ground Force* gardens would have been hard pushed to do without gravel. This chameleon-like material adapts to all sorts of uses and surroundings – as a cheap hard surface on its own, or spread between wide-spaced paving slabs to make a good-looking path, or around plants as a handsome and low-maintenance mulch. Warm in colour, it looks a treat with both buildings and plants. Gravel can be used to fill in odd corners around patios and buildings, saving you the tedious job of cutting bits of paving slabs to fit. And it makes a great surface on which to stand plants in containers, as there's no need to raise the pots off the ground so that the water drains away. As a side benefit, if you're concerned about security, gravel paths and driveways are strongly recommended by the police as it's well nigh impossible to walk silently over all those scrunching stones.

The key points to remember about gravel paths, drives and other areas is that they need a firm, weed-proof foundation, along with a raised edge to stop the stones escaping into lawns and borders. Areas that are likely to see lots of heavy use need a compacted hardcore foundation, varying from around 8–10cm (3–4in) for a path to 15–20cm (6–8in) for a driveway. Lay a weed-proof planting membrane over the soil in less-used areas. The choice of edging material depends on how visible the edge will be. One that will be covered by plants could be made of cheap reclaimed boards, for example, while terracotta edging tiles would look posh along a prominent edge.

A gravel mulch looks best around Mediterranean-type plants. As well as looking good it is also practical: it keeps down weeds, cuts down the amount of water that evaporates from the soil and provides good drainage around the stems of plants that like dry conditions.

Care and maintenance

If you've followed the advice given above when laying your gravel surface there should be very little in the way of maintenance, apart from an occasional raking to keep the gravel looking tidy and pulling up self-sown seedlings every now and then. However, if your gravel path or drive has been laid directly on to soil, weeds are likely to be a problem. Kill them either by spraying them with a path weedkiller, or take the chemical-free route of burning them off with a garden flame-thrower.

Toddlers absolutely adore gravel and spend hours sifting the stones, scrunching it with their feet and filling flowerpots. Put some sort of gravel area into your garden and it's virtually guaranteed to occupy tiny children for much longer than most toys will! Very young children will need supervision in case they put stones in their mouths, or they are not yet steady on their feet.

A combination of gravel and paving works well and is a cost-effective way of surfacing a large area.

how to lay paving round a pond

1 A 'collar' of mortar has been laid around the excavated hole of this pond to make a sound foundation, as the soil here is light and loose. A layer of sand is then placed over the mortar to protect the pond liner from sharp pieces.

2 The liner is tucked into the hole and the pond is filled with water. Then another layer of mortar is put down around the pond. The slabs are laid on the wet mortar with the edges sticking out over the rim of the pond in order to conceal the liner.

3 Use a spirit level to check that all the paving is level. This feature is being edged with bricks to provide a handsome finishing touch, and these are tapped firmly onto the wet mortar. Don't forget to check the levels here too.

Fences and fencing

The saying that 'good fences make good neighbours' tends to hold true for most people. After all, however well you get on with the folks next door, you probably don't want to see each other's every move, and nothing beats a fence for instant privacy. A fence topped off with trellis works well because it provides this without creating a closed-in feeling. The height of the trellis should be less than that of the fence: for example, a fence 1.2m (4ft) high plus trellis that is 30–60cm (12–24in) in height.

The most popular type of fence is made with overlapping panels. These come in a range of sizes and will last for a good few years, particularly if you make a really good job of putting them up. Closeboard fencing consists of vertical featheredged boards that are nailed so that they overlap each other. It is tough but also more expensive. To give your panels or boards

the best chance of staying free from rot, put a 'gravel board' along the bottom of each one. This is a treated plank or concrete panel and will protect the fence against knocks, and keep it off damp ground that would otherwise cause the timber to rot.

A fence can be dressed up or down depending on the wood stain you go for. Gone are the days when wood had to be some shade of brown – there's a fantastic range of coloured stains to suit every taste. Be careful when using creosote as it may cause damage to your plants or to you!

Fence posts are available in wood or concrete. Wood is cheaper but in the longer term it is likely to rot where the posts join the ground, while concrete is more expensive but will last for decades. However, some people don't like the look of concrete, regardless of how long it lasts. Never skimp the job of putting up the posts (see box, opposite) as wobbly ones are likely to result in a collapsed and broken fence.

Care and maintenance

Regular maintenance consists of treating the fence with wood stain or preservative every three years or so (see page 133). This is best done in autumn or early spring when the weather should be reasonably dry but when plants aren't growing strongly. Take care to do a thorough job and, if your neighbour allows you to, treat both sides of the fence.

Broken wooden posts are the most common problem. Check the fence in autumn and replace any posts that are on their way out. Rather than digging out an entire post and starting again, it's sometimes possible to saw off the rotten part and hammer a metal post support into the hole that was occupied by the old post. Otherwise, bolt on a concrete spur and sink it into a hole next to the existing post base.

Wooden fences should be thoroughly treated with wood stain before going up, and re-treated every three years.

other fencing ideas

Once upon a time a fence could just be made of wood, but recently there's been something of a revolution in the range of fences and screens available that can make an instant transformation to your garden. Screens like brushwood, bamboo or peeled reed can be bought in rolls or made into panels in a wooden frame. Woven hazel hurdles look wonderful in a country setting. Wooden fences now come in many different styles too – a far cry from ordinary overlap panels.

A brushwood screen can be used to hide these ordinary fence panels.

how to build a panel fence

The posts that support a fence need a firm foundation. At least a quarter of each post should be buried in the soil, bedded in concrete or put up using metal fencing spikes. For a concrete base, make a stiff mix of 1 part cement, 2.5 parts sand and 3.5 parts coarse aggregate.

Mark the line of the fence with string and pegs. Then, mark the position of each post using a bamboo cane cut to 1.9m (6ft 4in) to equal the width of a panel plus the thickness of a post. I would recommend using grooved fence posts as the fence panels can then just be slotted into place.

Put up two posts, using a spirit level to check they are vertical. At this point you can slot in gravel boards to protect the panels. Finally, slot the panel into place and fix it into position.

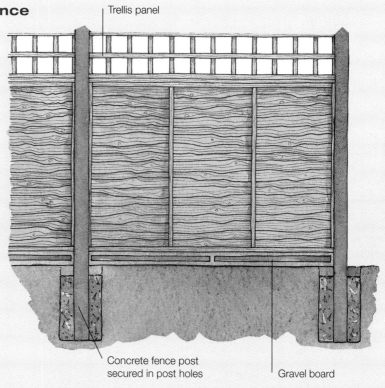

Trellis panel

Concrete fence post secured in post holes

Gravel board

Garden walls

Walls within gardens divide into two main types: dividing walls and retaining walls that support soil. Although brick is the first material that comes to mind there are plenty of others, including stone, open concrete blocks and railway sleepers. If you're lucky enough to have a tall boundary wall, take good care of it – large walls cost a fortune. For new walls more than several courses of bricks high you're probably better off calling in the professionals.

Low retaining walls are second to none when it comes to making sense out of an awkward, sloping site, as the soil can be levelled in a series of terraces. The number of levels depends on the lie of the land and the extent to which your garden slopes. When in doubt, go for several small retaining walls, each with a maximum height of around 45–60cm (18–24in), as wet soil is outrageously heavy. A solid brick or stone wall needs a really good foundation, about 45cm (18in) deep, and be sure to build in occasional drainage holes or 'weep holes' to let water run out. Railway sleepers are often the best DIY option as they are cheaper, quicker and easier to work with than brick or stone.

Retaining walls can also be used to create raised beds, either on a sloping site or on the level. A flat garden can be transformed by adding one or two of these beds. From a practical point of view, they are great news for anyone who finds bending a problem or who is in a wheelchair, as gardening becomes accessible again.

Walls create a wonderfully sheltered environment in which to grow exotic plants like tree ferns.

maintaining walls

The only maintenance required by most brick or stone walls is repointing old mortar that is starting to crumble. Scrape it out with a plugging chisel, or a cold chisel and hammer and use a pointed trowel to push in fresh mortar. Use a jointing iron, or a bent piece of copper pipe, to smooth it to a neat finish.

Right: Repointing old walls is a tedious but necessary job. Dig out all the crumbling mortar and replace it with a fresh mix.

PAINTING A WALL

Changing the colour of a wall can transform your garden. First, make sure the mortar is sound; if not, repoint as described above. Prepare the wall by cleaning off the surface using a stiff brush, and scrubbing off any patches of dirt. If the wall looks as though it has been liable to damp, paint it with a water-proofing solution, otherwise paint it with an exterior priming paint, then finish with the final coat of paint, which again should be one that is designed for outdoor use. Remember that the colour you decide upon will affect the look and feel of your garden, so choose with care.

ADDING A FENCE TO A WALL

Make a handsome boundary by building a low stone wall topped with a fence. This type of constuction is reasonably straightforward to build yourself, whereas a tall brick or stone wall is much trickier and is really a job for the professionals.

Before building the top 30cm (12in) of the wall, bed some fence posts into the mortar infill. Take care to space them at just the right distance apart. Leave the wall for a couple of days so the mortar sets hard, then put up the fence panels.

Below: A low wall can be made of stones, then topped with woven hurdles for privacy.

Garden buildings

SHEDS, SUMMERHOUSES AND GAZEBOS

All these buildings are generally made of wood, but to very different designs. While sheds are utilitarian in appearance and are usually tucked away and used purely for storage, gazebos and summerhouses are more decorative and are intended for relaxation. Gazebos are open-sided while summerhouses are completely enclosed.

Unless you splash out on a really expensive teak or cedar model, most garden buildings are made of softwood which is prone to rotting. So, be sure to buy one that has been pressure-treated with preservative and give it another coat of the same when you put it up. Most suppliers offer to 'dip' the panels for a small extra charge – which is a lot easier than doing it yourself – but the range of colours is likely to be very limited. Make sure the building is sited with a bit of space all round it so that you can paint it with wood preservative in the future.

A shed or summerhouse needs a firm foundation and is best put up on a 'raft' of solid concrete 15–30cm (6–12in) thick. A gazebo will only need such a foundation if it has a solid floor.

With a bit of ingenuity, there's no reason why one building can't serve two purposes. In a tiny garden you could pretty-up a shed with a coloured wood stain and add a pergola. A small deck would provide the perfect finishing touch – but you need to be an experienced decker before tackling something so tricky.

In a small garden, a shed cannot be hidden, but it can be cleverly blended with its surroundings.

With more people working from home, a summerhouse can make a practical office. One that is made for year-round use will cost a pretty penny, but will be a lot cheaper than moving to a more spacious house.

Care and maintenance

Buy tanalized wood that has been pressure-treated with preservative. If you saw through any planks during construction, paint the cut ends with timber preservative.

Wooden posts and structures need a fresh coat of preservative every couple of years. Pay particular attention to where the posts join the soil as this is where they are most susceptible to rot. Use a stiff hand-brush to remove dirt and algae and apply a coat of stain or preservative to all surfaces. If plants are growing on the structure, cut them back or remove them while you work – and choose preservative that won't harm them.

Treating timber takes a long time but mustn't be skimped on if your construction is going to last.

greenhouses

A greenhouse provides a marvellous environment for gardening under cover and even a tiny model will considerably enlarge the scope of what you can grow. There are numerous different models and designs, including lean-to types that can be placed against the house where space is limited. Site a greenhouse in a sunny spot and, if you want to heat it, with reasonable access to electricity too. Beware, though, greenhouse gardening can turn into a very absorbing hobby.

For the keen gardener, a greenhouse is the ultimate tool, where plants can be nurtured before outdoor planting.

JOBS FOR THE MONTH

spring march

Flower gardens
- Sow hardy annuals outside (see pages 78–9); frost-tender annuals must be sown under cover. Plant out autumn-sown sweet peas provided they have been hardened off.
- Early in the month, hard prune large-flowered types of clematis such as *C.* 'Jackmannii', and *C. viticella* varieties that flower in late summer (see page 67).
- To renovate deciduous shrubs that have become overgrown, hard prune them over a period of 2–3 years (see page 26).
- New growth is appearing on herbaceous perennials so cut back the dead stems if you didn't do this earlier. Divide and replant late-flowering perennials that have formed large, established clumps (see page 74).
- Trim overgrown ivies.

- Prune *Jasminum nudiflorum* (winter jasmine) once flowering has finished. Cut flowered shoots back to 2–3 buds.
- Prune roses as soon as possible this month (see page 27), with the exception of rambler roses that were pruned last summer. Delay until next month if the weather is very frosty.
- Shrubs to prune now include those that flower in late summer, such as buddleja (butterfly bush), those such as *Cornus alba* (dogwoods) that have coloured stems, and, towards the end of the month, lavatera (tree mallow). If necessary, trim evergreen shrubs including ilex (holly), ligustrum (privet), *Lonicera* 'Baggesen's Gold' and rhamnus (Italian buckthorn). See page 26.
- Trim winter-flowering heathers with shears once flowering is over.

Containers
- Buy ready-grown bulbs and pot them up to make an instant display.
- Scrub out used containers before planting in them.
- Trim off the dead stems of perennials and deciduous ornamental grasses at ground level before new growth appears.
- Top-dress (see page 95) or pot up permanent plants and lily bulbs before growth begins in earnest.

Lawns
- Begin mowing once the grass starts growing in earnest. Brush the lawn first to scatter wormcasts, using a stiff broom. Set the blades high for the first cut and lower them gradually to last year's level over the next two to three cuts.
- A new lawn can be made using either seed or turf (see pages 30 and 138).

Permanent container plants need top-dressing in spring with fresh compost and some controlled-release fertilizer.

- Scarify the lawn to remove the layer of dead grass or 'thatch' (see page 32).
- Spring is a good time to renovate a lawn (see page 33). Sow bare patches with fresh grass seed. Level out and repair bumps, hollows and broken edges.

Water features
- Start feeding fish once the weather begins to warm up, but take care not to overfeed them.
- Put pumps that were removed and stored for winter back in the water.
- Feed water plants with tablets of aquatic plant fertilizer.

Under cover
- Ready grown young seeding plants and starter plants or 'tots' are on sale now. Pot up starter plants into 7.5cm (3in) pots and prick out seedlings into trays. Grow them on in a warm, well-lit environment.

All garden plants benefit from a feed of slow-release fertilizer in spring, along with a mulch on bare soil.

- Half-hardy annuals can be sown under cover for growing on in a heated greenhouse or on a warm window sill. In an unheated greenhouse, sow hardy annuals in modular trays for an early display of flowers.
- Greenhouse vegetables can be sown now. However, if you only want a handful of plants, there should be plenty of ready-grown ones on sale.
- Tender perennials that have been overwintered under cover should now be coming into growth and cuttings can be taken from the new shoots.

General
- Feed all garden plants with a general slow-release fertilizer. Roses benefit from special rose fertilizer.
- Mulch borders while the ground is damp and free from weeds, and before plants begin to grow strongly.
- Control weeds with regular hoeing or hand-weeding or they'll quickly get out of hand.
- Paint wooden buildings, supports and fences or treat them with wood preservative as soon as possible, before plant growth establishes.

Flower gardens

- Regularly tie in the new growth on climbing plants and wall shrubs while the stems are young and flexible.
- Cut back deciduous shrubs by half, like cotinus (smoke bush) and sambucus (golden elder) that have coloured foliage.
- Thin out evergreen shrubs that have become overgrown.
- Cut back frost-damaged shoots on evergreens to healthy growth.
- Cut back last year's growth on fuchsias (hardy varieties) to about 5cm (2in).
- Sow hardy annuals outdoors where they are to flower (see page 78). This can be done until the end of the month.
- Use stakes to support herbaceous perennials that will eventually grow tall.

- Slugs and snails tend to feast on new plant growth. Protect susceptible plants like hostas and lilies as soon as the first spears of foliage appear.
- Shrubs to prune include lavender, santolina, and *Spiraea* × *bumalda* varieties.
- Give topiary plants like box, bay and holly their first light trim of the year.

Containers

- Bulbs that have finished flowering can be kept for next year if they are deadheaded, then fed and watered until the foliage has yellowed and died back.
- Pot frost-tender plants into their final containers such as tubs, window boxes or hanging baskets, provided they can be kept in a frost-free place like a porch, greenhouse or conservatory for another month or so.

make a lawn from turf

1 Prepare the ground thoroughly by digging it over, removing weeds and raking it level. Tread over the soil to firm it down, then rake again.

2 Buy good quality turf and lay it within a couple of days of delivery. Put each turf in place and pat it down with your hands. If you need to stand on the lawn, use a plank to spread your weight.

3 Stagger the joints, like those in brickwork, and make sure all the turves are butted close together without any cracks showing. During dry spells, keep the lawn well watered until established.

- Plant up flower pouches (see page 88) using 'starter' or 'plug' plants, provided the pouches can be kept under cover for another month or so.
- Herbs may need potting up to the next size of container.
- Buy and pot up lily bulbs for summer flowers.
- Feed strawberries with a general liquid feed.
- Buy and plant tomatoes that will be grown under cover (see page 97).
- Water more frequently as the weather warms up.

Lawns

- Feed established lawns with a spring lawn fertilizer.
- Mow regularly from now onwards, usually once or twice a week.
- New lawns can be made with seed or turf (see pages 30 and 138), though the job is best completed by the end of the month when the weather tends to become warmer and drier.
- Treat weeds with a lawn weedkiller.

Water features

- Clean out ponds if necessary (see page 103). Only do this once every 5–7 years, unless the water is obviously polluted.
- Green water often occurs in spring. Once existing pond plants are growing strongly they usually solve the problem. Otherwise, add new ones following the instructions for 'How to plant a pond' (see page 110–11).
- Divide marginal pond plants as for herbaceous perennials (see page 74) and water lilies (see page 108) if they are forming large, overgrown clumps.
- Give pebbles or cobbles on small moving-water features a good scrub to get rid of green algae.

Under cover

- Annual climbers like ipomoea (morning glory) and *Cobaea scandens* (cup-and-saucer plant) can be sown now.
- Greenhouse vegetables can be planted out into growing bags.
- Hanging baskets, flower pouches and containers can

Sometimes spring can seem to take a long time in coming, but these Regal Pelargoniums, grown in the greenhouse, will brighten up any cold, wet day.

be planted up now with frost-tender bedding plants, so long as there is enough space to grow them under cover in a heated environment.
- Frost-tender vegetables like runner beans, marrows, courgettes and squashes can be sown in pots.
- Frost-tender herbs like basil can be sown in pots.
- Winter-flowering pansies can be sown now.

General

- Plant evergreen shrubs that are on the tender side, such as ceanothus, choisya and phormium. The same goes for hedges of box, golden privet, holly and laurel.
- Formally shaped hedges that will probably need pruning include Leyland cypress, Lawson's cypress, privet and laurel (see pages 24–5).
- Set up a water butt to save water for the summer (see page 23).

spring may

Flower gardens

- Thin out annuals that were sown outside so that there is 10cm (4in) between plants. Transplant surplus seedlings to fill gaps elsewhere.
- Sow biennials in an out-of-the-way corner for flowers next spring and summer.
- Regularly tie in climbers, especially clematis and sweet peas, or they'll get into a real tangle.
- If *Clematis montana* varieties need pruning do this immediately after flowering. Prune *C. alpina* and *C. macropetala* if overgrown. (See page 67.)
- Sow half-hardy annuals outdoors where they are to flower.
- Spray roses that have previously suffered from diseases like blackspot as a preventative measure.

- Cut back outward-growing shoots on wall-trained chaenomeles (flowering quince) and pyracantha (firethorn) to two buds, once flowering has finished.
- Remove spring bedding plants from borders and beds as soon as they begin to fade.

Containers

- Feed and water bulbs that have flowered until their leaves yellow and die back.
- Herbs do well if planted now and should be on sale in a good range of varieties, including annuals. If you make a lot of use of popular herbs like basil and parsley, it's worth growing your own from seed.
- Buy frost-tender plants and plant them outside towards the end of the month. First harden off any plants that have been growing under cover.
- Bring outside again permanent, frost-tender plants that were moved indoors for the winter.
- Pests to watch out for and treat if necessary include slugs, snails and vine weevil (see page 34–5).
- Feed strawberries with a liquid tomato fertilizer when the flowers appear and continue until the fruit begins to ripen.
- Plant tomato plants for growing outside towards the end of the month.

Lawns

- New lawns that were made last month should be ready for their first cut. Roll the grass with the roller on the back of the mower, then cut it a couple of days later with the blades set at their highest level.
- Water new lawns during dry spells, preferably in the early morning or the evening.
- Feed an established lawn, if you've not already done so.

Spring is the ideal time for planting herbs, and there should be a good selection of plants on sale now.

Water features

- Pull out blanket weed in a pond by hand; or tackle the problem with pads of straw or lavender stalks (see page 101). Make sure the pond is well planted.
- Container ponds can go back outside, or be refilled.
- Feed fish once a day, but only with as much food as they can eat in about ten minutes.
- Plant pond plants like marginals and water lilies so that they have plenty of time to establish before winter.
- Clean out the pond, but only if really necessary. Small ponds need a major clean-out every three to five years, large ones every five to seven years. The exception is if the water is obviously polluted and looks black or smells awful. If there is a lot of blanket weed or if algae have formed floating scums, some action will be needed (see page 103).
- Water lilies that are about six or seven years old and marginal plants that are over five can be divided and replanted to improve performance (see page 108).

Under cover

- Make regular sowings of herbs, like parsley, to be sure of a continuous supply.
- Finish planting greenhouse vegetables. Support plants like cucumbers with canes, while tomatoes do best if trained up strings that are secured under the rootballs when planting.
- Tender shrubs and perennials that have been overwintering under cover can now go back outside, unless the weather is unseasonably cold. First, acclimatize them to the outside world by standing them out for increasing periods of time before they go out permanently.
- Annuals will need to be hardened off before going outside at the end of the month when all danger of frost is past. A cold frame is ideal for the job as the lid can be left open for increasing periods of time, which will save you carrying plants in and out for a couple of weeks.

New plants need to be kept well-watered during any dry spells, for their first spring and summer.

- Pests and diseases can start to take hold as the weather warms up. Inspect plants regularly – squashing small infestations by hand can be sufficient. Putting up yellow 'sticky traps' also helps monitor which pests are flying around.
- Outdoor vegetables can still be sown under cover in pots to shorten the overall growing time. (See April.)

General

- Hedges of berberis, elaeagnus, griselinia and *Viburnum tinus* may need pruning if they have become overgrown or straggly.
- Make sure that new plants are watered thoroughly during dry spells.
- Weeds are growing fast now and will need controlling little and often. Spring is one of the best times to apply systemic weedkillers, while contact types can be applied from spring to autumn.

summer june

Flower gardens
- Bulbs growing in grass should have died back and the area can be mown.
- Regularly tie in climbers.
- Prune deciduous shrubs like philadelphus (mock orange blossom) and weigela that have just finished flowering (see page 26).
- Cut out the flowered stems of euphorbias at or near to ground level when the flowers start looking brown and tatty. Protect your skin from the milky sap as it can cause irritation.
- Continue thinning out overgrown evergreens.
- Deadhead rhododendrons, but take care not to damage new shoots.
- Rose bushes should be checked for suckers – shoots that come from the ground near the base of the plant. Dig back to the main stem and pull off the shoot rather than cutting it.

- Rambler roses should be tied in regularly before their stems harden.
- Tree ferns need to be watered daily during warm, dry weather. Using a hose, let the water overflow the crown (the top of the trunk) and run down the trunk to soak it thoroughly.

Containers
- Continue planting all types of containers with summer-flowering annuals and tender perennials.
- Feed all plants in containers, starting about six weeks after potting when the fertilizer in the compost will have run out. The exception is if a controlled-release fertilizer, which will last until late summer, was added earlier.
- Use stakes to support lilies that grow tall.
- Strawberries should be ripening now. Inspect the fruits regularly and pick off any that are turning brown or mouldy as they'll infect others.
- Tie in tomatoes regularly as the stems grow. Remove sideshoots as they appear, except in bushy varieties.
- Water all pots regularly and never let them dry out. If you plan to set up a drip system for automatic watering when you're on holiday, install it in plenty of time so that you can be sure it works well (see page 84).
- Lilies should be inspected regularly for lily beetle. The adult beetles are bright red and the orangey grubs surround themselves with black slime.

Lawns
- If grass is beginning to look tired and yellow feed it with a liquid fertilizer.
- Mow less often during dry spells and raise the height of the mower blades. Longer grass is less likely to scorch in the sun.
- Keep perennial weeds under control by raking with a springtine rake before mowing. This brings up the runners which are then chopped off by the mower.

Put up supports for climbing plants and tall perennials – preferably before there is too much growth to cope with.

An arbour is the perfect place to relax and take a brief rest from all your gardening exertions.

Water features
- Introduce new fish to the pond now that the water has warmed up.
- Thin out oxygenating plants that are growing vigorously (see page 110).
- Clean pump filters every week or so, particularly if a pump is being run a lot.
- Buy tender floating plants like water hyacinth and put them in the pond.
- Plants should be growing strongly and any green water should have become clear. There's still time to add new plants if necessary so that they can become well established before winter. Other than that, there's little to do apart from sit back and enjoy your pond.
- Water loss is common in hot weather. Set up a water butt to collect rainwater for topping up the pond, rather than using tap water which is rich in mineral salts that provide food for green algae.

Under cover
- All tender flowering plants and vegetables can now be planted outside, but do harden them off first (see May).
- Grow some plants for next autumn and winter. Raise your own pot plants by sowing seed of browallia, cineraria and schizanthus (poor man's orchid). When the seedlings are large enough to handle, prick out into 7.5cm (3in) pots.
- Ornamental cabbages and kale can be sown now to brighten your containers next autumn. Sow the seeds individually in 7.5cm (3in) pots.
- Keep tomatoes well watered as variations in supply can result in fruit split. Begin feeding with a liquid fertilizer. Remove the sideshoots as they appear.

General
- Late frosts may still occur, so it's worth having horticultural fleece to hand to cover newly planted tender plants if necessary.
- Water all new plants during dry spells.
- Weed regularly. Hoeing during hot weather is effective.

summer july

Flower gardens

- Sow biennial flowers such as forget-me-nots, sweet rocket and wallflowers by the end of the month if you want to raise plants from seed.
- Cut back herbaceous perennials like herbaceous geraniums and oriental poppies that may have flowered and then flopped over to ground level, to encourage neat, new growth.
- Deadhead sweet peas as they will stop flowering if the seed pods remain.
- Now is the time to give any topiary plants a second trim.

Containers

- Deadhead flowering plants regularly to encourage more flowers.
- Herbs benefit from a regular trim to keep growth neat and bushy.
- Trim all old leaves and fruit stems off strawberries once fruiting has finished, to make way for the new leaves. Do this as soon as possible as trimming allows next year's fruit-producing shoots to grow properly.

Plants in small beds need an occasional soaking during dry weather.

paving for all seasons

Summer is a good time to tackle major projects such as paving. However, remember that your path or patio has to survive the winter months too, so make sure you build it on good solid foundations and always allow a slight slope across the finished surface for drainage.

Fill the gaps in paving with a dry mix of three parts soft sand to one part cement.

- Keep tomatoes evenly watered as extremes of moisture cause the fruit to split.
- Water frequently in hot weather, as often as twice a day for containers like hanging baskets in exposed spots. Try to water first thing in the morning and in the evening, when the sun won't scorch wet plants. An automatic watering system is wonderful for doing the watering at anti-social times.

Water features

- Blanket weed grows strongly in summer so pull it out by hand on a regular basis.
- Evaporation during hot weather causes water levels to fall sharply. Top up a pond, ideally with rainwater, and remember to check the level in covered moving-water features.
- Pests like greenfly sometimes attack pond plants. Fish and other creatures will usually eat them if you weigh down the leaves for a day or two.
- Check water lilies occasionally for signs of pests or diseases. Thin out growth with secateurs if the leaves are overcrowded (see page 108).

General

- Trim conifer hedges.
- Turn the compost heap to speed up rotting.

- Target water-use during long dry spells by concentrating on those plants that need it most, like those that are newly planted.

When watering, take care not to splash plant foliage if the sun is shining or large, glossy leaves could become scorched.

summer august

Flower gardens
- Gather up diseased leaves and flowers and put them in the bin to avoid spreading infection.
- Trim the dead flower stems off lavender and santolina. Give the entire plants a light trim at the same time.
- Prune rambler roses as soon as flowering has finished (see page 27).
- Prune wisteria by cutting sideshoots to 15cm (6in).

Containers
- Buy and plant chrysanthemums which will flower until the first frosts.
- Feed containers planted with seasonal summer flowers with a liquid feed once a week. This also applies to those fed with controlled-release fertilizer earlier in the year.

- Harvest and dry or freeze herbs for winter use.
- Pinch out the tops of tomatoes once four fruiting shoots have formed. Remove sideshoots as they appear.

Water features
- Fish need lots of oxygen in hot weather so keep the fountain running as much as possible. If fish are 'gasping' near the surface of the pond, spray it with a jet of water as a temporary measure.
- Thin out pond plants that have made lots of growth. Try to cut rather than pull out their leaves if possible.

Harvest vegetables like runner beans regularly. This will ensure cropping right until the end of the season.

Under cover

- Greenhouse vegetables should be fed twice a week with a liquid fertilizer.
- Continue to train tomatoes and to remove sideshoots as they appear.
- Ventilate the greenhouse all day, and all night if the weather is hot. Spray the floor with water to keep the atmosphere humid.
- Take cuttings of tender perennials.

General

- Trim formal hedges (see pages 24–5). These include beech, holly, lavender and yew. Informal hedges that may need pruning include escallonia and pyracantha.
- Virus diseases often become obvious in late summer. Watch out for yellow or white mottling or streaking on leaves, and destroy infected plants.

Stop feeding permanent plants in containers, as this encourages soft growth that could be damaged by frost.

how to pot up a pot plant

1 Large well-grown plants make instant specimens for containers. First remove the pot – it may be necessary to cut it off rather than just knocking the plant out of its container.

2 Put a good layer of drainage material in the base of the container and put in some soil-based potting compost.

3 Before planting, tease out some of the largest roots to encourage them to grow outwards into the new soil.

autumn september

Flower gardens
- Transplant, or buy and plant biennials as soon as possible.
- Plant bulbs including daffodils, narcissi, crocus and snowdrops by the end of the month (see pages 76–7). Delay planting tulips until October or November.
- Sow hardy annuals where they are to flower provided the soil is well drained (see pages 78–9). On heavy soils, sow in spring.
- Sow sweet peas in pots and keep them outside over winter in a cold frame, or protected by a cloche or pane of glass.

Containers
- Plant autumn bedding plants like cyclamen, *Erica gracilis* and winter cherry as soon as containers become available. Site containers in a sheltered spot.
- Plant daffodil and narcissi bulbs, plus early flowering ones such as winter aconites and crocus by the end of the month (see pages 92–3).
- Plant permanent plants for autumn and winter containers so that they become established before the cold weather (see pages 90–1).
- Plant strawberries to ensure a reasonable crop next year (see page 96).

Lawns
- Autumn is an excellent time to make new lawns from seed or turf (see pages 30 and 138).
- If an established lawn wasn't fed in spring, feed it now with an autumn lawn fertilizer.
- Lawns should be mown less frequently now. Raise the height of the blades to about 2.5cm (1in).
- Rake out the 'thatch' or dead grass (see page 32).

Only plant potentially tender evergreens, like this bay tree, in autumn if the site is very sheltered.

Water features
- Empty small container ponds that are above ground, or move them under cover complete with plants. Put fish in a tank in a frost-free place.
- Bring frost-tender floating aquatic plants indoors.
- Fish need less food as the temperature falls.
- Sediment is almost certain to have built up on the floor of the pond. Use a fine-mesh net to scoop out most of it, but leave about 2.5–5cm (1–2in) behind.

Under cover
- Greenhouse heaters should be cleaned and checked over in readiness for winter.
- Herbs can be potted up and moved under cover to provide plenty of fresh leaves for winter use.
- Sow hardy annuals in pots or modular trays for a really early show of flowers next spring and summer.

Leave the final cut until spring

While the idea of an autumn tidy-up is a traditional one for many gardeners, it's actually a much better idea to delay cutting back perennial plants until spring. On a practical level, the dead growth provides useful frost protection for the plants and valuable winter shelter for insects, like ladybirds and lacewings, that are an enormous help in pest control. From an ornamental point of view, as soon as the frosty weather arrives, your garden will be turned into a magical winter wonderland with all the plant stems silvered with frost.

- Give the greenhouse a good clean-out ready for winter. Move plants outside where possible, remove the shading, clean out gutters and wash the glass inside and out. Dry and store capillary matting as it'll make the atmosphere too humid in winter. It may also be worth fumigating the greenhouse to keep pests and diseases under control.
- While the greenhouse is empty, it's well worth insulating it with bubble polythene.

General
- Autumn is the best time for planting all hardy plants, except on heavy soils. The main exception is evergreens that may be susceptible to frost damage and are best planted in spring.
- Moving established plants is best done in autumn. First prepare a plant's new site, then transplant it and keep it well watered.
- Apply systemic weedkillers to persistent perennial weeds. Do this as soon as possible while the plants are growing strongly.

Once late-blooming plants have finished flowering, leave dead stems on for the winter in order to provide protection for beneficial insects.

- If necessary, treat wooden features, furniture and buildings with wood stain or preservative while the weather is still fairly dry.
- Rake up fallen leaves at regular intervals, particularly if they're on the lawn or border. Compost small amounts and put larger quantities in dustbin bags to rot down into leaf mould within a year or so. See page 15.
- Dig over clay soil before the weather becomes too wet, and leave it rough over winter for the frost to break down.
- Give dirty or mossy paving a good scrub with paving cleaner or the surface may become dangerously slippery.
- Hedges of Lawson's cypress and yew may need an autumn trim (see page 24–5).
- Plant hardy plants, provided the soil isn't soaking wet.

autumn october

Flower gardens
- Plant biennials as soon as possible.
- Plant all bulbs by the end of October, with the exception of tulips which can be planted up to the end of November (see pages 76–7).
- Lift, divide and replant perennials that flower in early to mid-summer and that have formed large clumps (see page 74). Late-flowering ones can be left until spring.
- Conifers, evergreen trees and shrubs can be planted now.
- Lift and pot up tender perennials and overwinter them in a frost-free place.
- Tender bulbs and tubers, like dahlias and gladioli, should be lifted and stored before the first hard frost if you want to keep them for next year. In mild areas, dahlias often survive if covered with a layer of mulch.

Containers
- Move bulbs in pots to a sheltered, fairly dry spot like the base of a house wall.
- Perennials and deciduous ornamental grasses die back to ground level in autumn but the dead growth is best left on to give a bit of frost protection.
- Move shrubs like bay, cordyline, phormium and tree ferns, which are frost-tender in cold areas, into a porch, greenhouse or conservatory. If the only option is to leave them outside, make 'jackets' of bubble polythene to slip over cordyline and tree ferns in case there are very cold spells, and buy horticultural fleece to protect the others.

Lawns
- Improve drainage if the lawn stays wet for any length of time after rain (see page 33).
- Finish seeding or turfing new lawns by the end of the month (see pages 33 and 138).

Water features
- Cover the pond with a net before leaves start to fall and leave it covered for a couple of months.
- Give fish less and less food as the weather becomes colder. Don't feed them at all over winter.
- Cut back marginal plants to just above water level once the foliage has yellowed and died back. Completely remove water-lily foliage that has died back.
- If a pump is in shallow water or won't be used over winter, take it out and scrub it in clean water, then dry and store it for the winter. Put a pond heater in its place if there are fish in the pond.
- Scoop out sediment that has gathered on the floor of the pond with a fine net.

Autumn is the best time for planting all hardy plants (except on heavy soils), as they'll have plenty of time to establish before bursting into growth next year.

Under cover

- Watering should be reduced now the weather is becoming colder.
- Ventilate as much as the weather permits and always remember to space plants well apart to avoid potential problems with grey mould or botrytis, as good air movement helps prevent disease. Remove any dead or faded leaves or flowers every couple of days.

General

- Dig over clay soil before the weather becomes too wet, and leave it rough over winter for the frost to break down.
- Drain watering systems and equipment and store them under cover for the winter.

Right: Trim back plants overhanging your boundary before the autumn gales arrive.

Above: Give the lawn a final cut in autumn with the mower blades set high, so it will stay tidy for winter.

winter november/december

Flower gardens
- To prevent wind damage, prune by half tall shrubs like butterfly bush and tree mallow that will be pruned next spring.
- Plant tulips until the end of November (see pages 76–7).
- Plant winter-flowering pansies by the end of November.

Containers
- Move bulbs to a sheltered spot if you haven't done so earlier. Tulips can still be planted.
- Protect permanent plants, particularly evergreens, from frost during very cold spells.
- Stand any container-grown plants against the walls of your house when the weather gets cold. When you are expecting a very heavy frost lag the pots with old sacking or bubble polythene.

- Empty pots that aren't frost-proof and store them over winter. First, give them a good scrub inside and out using hot water.
- Occasional watering may be necessary during winter, but check the compost first and only water sparingly.

Lawns
- Watch out for areas of the lawn that may become waterlogged and make a note to improve the drainage next spring.
- Avoid walking on the lawn while the grass is frozen, or you could create some unsightly yellow patches.

Water features
- If your pump is in the pond run it for a short time every couple of weeks to prevent it seizing up.

cleaning garden tools

1 Although it may seem like a dull job, give your tools a bit of tender loving care before putting them away for winter, so they'll be all ready for next year. Use emery paper to remove dried sap from shears and secateurs.

2 Sharpen the blades of hoes, as well as secateurs and shears. Use a file on the hoe blade.

3 Rub down wooden handles with a cloth soaked in linseed oil. Clean metal parts with an oily rag.

- A solid layer of ice that lasts for more than a couple of days is dangerous to a pond's inhabitants so keep a small area ice-free (see page 113).

Under cover
- Tender shrubs and perennials that have been moved into an unheated greenhouse are best watered very sparingly during winter.
- Pot up a few early-flowering perennials like primulas, polyanthus and lily-of-the-valley and bring them under cover to make a lovely show of flowers after Christmas.
- Heating is usually essential now if you want to keep the greenhouse frost-free. Insulating with bubble polythene will help cut heating bills.
- Continue to ventilate the greenhouse whenever the weather allows.
- Keep a look out for pests like vine weevil, which can thrive in a heated greenhouse. Also watch out for mice which look for shelter under cover and may feast on bulbs.
- Clean used pots and seed trays with hot water and disinfectant, ready for use next spring.

General
- Birds appreciate a supply of food and water over winter, but they will eventually come to depend on it, so only start feeding them if you'll be able to do so regularly.
- Borders can be tidied up any time during winter provided the soil isn't wet. Pull up dead annuals, cut back the dead stems of perennials and grasses, pull out weeds, rake up fallen leaves and lightly fork over the bare soil between plants.
- Newly planted conifers and evergreens are susceptible to damage from cold winds and may need protecting with windbreak netting.
- Garden furniture is best stored in the shed or garage for the winter. Protect anything that has to stay outside with plastic covers.
- Hard prune hedges of deciduous plants that have become overgrown.

- Check new plants every week or so and firm them in if their roots have been loosened by wind or frost. Check that tree stakes and ties are still secure and that they aren't rubbing the trunk. You can continue planting provided the ground isn't wet or frozen.
- Put up supports for climbing plants while there is less plant growth to contend with.
- Bird boxes should be cleaned of old nesting material and scrubbed out with plain boiling water without any detergent. Let the box dry, then put in a handful of dry grass or hay for birds, like wrens, that may use it as a winter roost.
- Buy in manure and stack it.
- Move garden ornaments that may be damaged by frost into a shed or other sheltered position.

Protect the crowns of tree ferns from winter cold by lagging them with straw or bracken.

winter january/february

Flower gardens
- Cut the old leaves off *Helleborus orientalis* (Lenten rose) so that they don't spoil the effect of the flowers.
- Prune roses towards the end of February in mild areas (see page 27).
- In January, cut back to 2–3 buds the shoots on wisteria that were pruned last summer.

Containers
- Water sparingly if the compost is drying out.
- Towards the end of February, permanent plants can be top-dressed with a little fresh potting compost.
- Herbaceous perennials and grasses that have formed large clumps can be split and repotted towards the end of February (see page 74).

Lawns
- Aerate the lawn (see page 33).
- Give the lawn its first cut if the weather is mild and dry and growth has started early. Brush the grass first to scatter worm casts and mow the lawn with the blades set at their highest level.

Water features
- Keep a small area of the pond ice-free during freezing weather (see page 113).
- If your pump is in the pond run it for a short while every fortnight.

Frost brings a touch of magic to the garden and shows the worth of not cutting back dead stems until spring.

Under cover

- Lettuce can be sown in an unheated greenhouse or cold frame, using a variety that has been bred for winter sowing.
- Hardy annuals can be sown in an unheated greenhouse to produce an early summer crop of flowers.
- Lily bulbs can be bought and potted up in an unheated greenhouse during February to get off to a flying start. Plants can go outside in later spring.
- Continue ventilating as much as possible and keep plants spaced well apart to prevent fungal diseases.
- Buy and pot-up tubers of begonias and grow them on in a warm place to have your own flowering pot plants.
- Tomatoes can be sown in February if you plan to grow them in a heated greenhouse.
- Keep the glass in your greenhouse as clean and snow-free as possible. This will make sure that the maximum amount of light will reach your young plants and seedlings.

General

- Send your lawnmower for servicing while it isn't needed.
- Clean paths and patios of moss and dirt or they'll become dangerously slippery.
- Large quantities of snow can damage plants and garden structures, so use a broom to knock off the worst of it.
- Look at the bare bones of your garden and decide what could be changed next year.
- Treat wooden fences, supports and structures that are only accessible when plant growth dies back, with wood preservative.
- Prepare ground for early sowings of flower or vegetable seed by covering it with clear polythene for several weeks first. This will warm the soil and get seeds off to a flying start.
- If conditions are not too wet, dig over and prepare the ground for planting or ready for a new lawn during February. Ground that was rough-dug in autumn, with the soil left in large clods, can be broken down with a fork.

Time to put the garden to bed, then sit in the warm and make plans for next year.

- Start your new compost heap in a hidden corner of the garden. Well-rotted compost will always come in extremely handy in the spring.
- Check your paths, patios, fences and gates for any damage that might have occurred throughout the year. Take this opportunity to make thorough repairs and carry out any general maintenance that might be necessary.
- Now is the time to select your seeds for the spring. Contact mail-order companies for catalogues and carefully fill in the order form. When your seeds arrive make sure that you store them in a cool and dry environment.
- Take a trip to your local garden centre during this quiet time and keep your eyes peeled for any seasonal bargains. You can get ahead of the game by buying all your requirements for the coming season in one go.
- Tools need an occasional sort-out and now is a good time to tidy the shed, clean and oil equipment, and sharpen secateurs and shears (see page 152).

Stockists and suppliers

PAINT
Akzo Nobel Woodcare
St Ives, Cambridgeshire
01480 496868

Charles Bentley & Son (paintbrushes)
Loughborough, Leicestershire
01509 232757

Hammerite Products Ltd
Prudhoe, Northumberland
01661 830000

HMG Coatings (South) Ltd
Andover, Hampshire
01264 333770

PAVING
Blanc de Bierges (slabs and bricks)
Peterborough, Cambridgeshire
01733 202566

Bradstone (paving, walling, driveways)
Ashbourne, Derbyshire
01335 372255

Harveys Sand and Gravel
Swindon, Gloucestershire
01793 643744

Hidden Edge Systems (paving, rails)
Exeter, Devon
01392 436290

Jewsons (builders merchant, tool hire)
Coventry, West Midlands
02476 438400

Marshalls (Yorkstone Circle Paving)
Halifax, West Yorkshire
01422 306300

Michelmersh (bricks and tiles)
Romsey, Hampshire
01794 368506

Park Products (slab lifter)
Blackburn, Lancashire
01254 614000

Pentagon (Jersey) Wholesale Limited
St Saviour, Channel Islands
01534 888000

Pinks Hill Landscape Merchants
Guildford, Surrey
01483 571620

Ryburn Rubber Ltd (rubber flagstones)
Sowerby Bridge, West Yorkshire
01422 316323

Stonemarket (paving)
Ryton-on-Dunsmore, Warwickshire
02476 305530

Town and Country Paving Ltd
Littlehampton, West Sussex
01903 776297

Travis Perkins
Northampton
01604 752424

Wavin Plastics Limited
(Italian circular paving)
Chippenham, Wiltshire
01249 766600

PLANTS
Barcham Trees Plc (container trees)
Ely, Cambridgeshire
01353 720748

Bernhard's Nurseries Ltd
(trees and shrubs)
Rugby, Warwickshire
01788 521177

British Wild Flower Plants
North Burlington, Norfolk
01603 716615

Capital Gardens,
Alexandra Palace, London
020 8444 2555

Chapel Cottage Plants
Nr March, Cambridgeshire
01354 740938

Deepdale Trees Limited
Sandy, Bedfordshire
01767 262636

Dobbies Garden World
Lasswade, Midlothian
0131 6631941

Emorsgate Seeds (wildflower seeds)
Kings Lynn, Norfolk
01553 829028

Garden Style (specimen plants)
Farnham, Surrey
01252 735331

Langley Boxwood Nursery
(box plants and topiary)
Nr Liss, Hampshire
01730 894467

Layham Garden Centre and Nursery
(herbaceous plants and roses)
Canterbury, Kent
01304 813267

Millbrook Garden Company
Gravesend, Kent
01474 331135

Notcutts Garden Centres
Bagshot, Surrey
01276 472288

Pantiles Plant and Garden Centre
Chertsey, Surrey
01932 872195

Ransoms Garden Centre
St Martin, Jersey
01534 856699

Summerhill Nurseries Ltd
Billericay, Essex
01268 521052

Tendercare
Denham, Middlesex
01895 835544

Wyevale Garden Centres Plc
Hereford
01635 873700

POTS
Capital Garden Products Ltd
Ticehurst, East Sussex
01580 201092

Cesol Tiles Ltd (terracotta ovens)
Wallingford, Oxfordshire
01491 833662

Ceramica de Catalunya (garden pots)
Henley-on-Thames, Oxfordshire
01491 628994

C H Brannam Ltd
Barnstaple, North Devon
01271 343035

Grenadier Fire Lighters Ltd
Chester, Cheshire
01829 741649

Iguana (Chiminea)
London
020 8543 5629

J G S Design (ceramic jugs and pots)
Birmingham, West Midlands
Tel: 0121 7078200

Megaceramics UK Ltd
Louth, Lincolnshire
01507 601000

Pots and Pithoi (terracotta pots)
Turners Hill, West Sussex
01342 714793

Sandford Stone (garden stoneware)
Winscombe, Somerset
01934 823591

Spanish Rings Ltd
(Spanish wall pot-holders)
East Molesey, Surrey
020 8224 9381

Tom Critchley (Portuguese and Turkish
handmade pots)
07785 995349

Whichford Pottery (terracotta pots)
Nr Shipston on Stour, Warwickshire
01608 684416

STRUCTURES
Cotswold Decorative Ironworkers Ltd
(metal arbours)
Stourton, Warwickshire
01608 685134

Dillons Garden Sheds Ltd (playhouses)
Southampton, Hampshire
02380 873787

Garden Images Ltd (sundials)
Solihull, West Midlands
01564 794035

Haddonstone Ltd (urns and sundials)
Northampton
01604 770711

Halls Garden Products Ltd (glasshouses)
Aylesford, Kent
01622 791234

MPA Leisure Buildings Ltd (Glasshouse)
Chesterfield, Derbyshire
0800 318359

J L Newman and Son Ltd
Swaffham Bulbeck, Cambridgeshire
01223 812729

E H Thorne (beehives)
Market Rasen, Lincolnshire
01673 858555

Windrush Willows
(woven willow structures)
Witney, Oxfordshire
01993 709317

SURFACES
A H Allen Steel Services Ltd
(metal flooring)
Northampton
01604 762211

Border Hardcore and Rockery Stone
Company Ltd (Pebbles and cobbles)
Welshpool, Powys
01938 570375

J Arthur Bower's (compost and bark)
Lincoln
01522 537561

Brick and Stone (Scotland) Ltd
(rockery stone)
Edinburgh
0131 551 1155

Davidson and Muirson Ltd
(stone and topsoil)
Aberdeen
01224 782700

ECO Composting Ltd
(recycled landscaping products)
Christchurch, Dorset
01202 593601

Rolawn Ltd (washed turf)
York, North Yorkshire
01904 608661

Westland Horticulture (play bark)
Dungannon, County Tyrone
028 8772 7500

TIMBER
Archadeck (American timber decks)
Gainsborough, Lincolnshire
01427 616400

T Chamber and Son Ltd
(tanalized timber)
Stratford, London
020 8534 6318

Coastal Lumber Company
Bishop's Stortford, Hertfordshire
01279 652121

G E Collis and Sons Ltd
Burntwood, Staffordshire
01543 686370

Dandf Jardine (gazebos)
Pontefract, West Yorkshire
01977 704796

Deck-It (custom-built decks)
Walgrave, Northamptonshire
01604 781833

Deckor Timber
Harrogate, North Yorkshire
01423 527505

Forest Garden (trellis and fences)
Nr Worcester
01886 812451

Hillhout Ltd (trellis)
Beccles, Suffolk
01502 718091

H S Jackson & Son (Fencing) Ltd
(machine-rounded posts)
Ashford, Kent
01233 750393

Outdoor Deck Company
Sheen, London
020 8876 8464

Redwood Decking Ltd
Formby, Merseyside
01704 832355

Snows Timber (timber merchant)
Andover, Hampshire
01264 735371

Ternex Ltd (hardwood decking)
Welwyn, Hertfordshire
01707 324606

M & M Timber Company Ltd
(machine-rounded timber)
Nr Kidderminster, Worcestershire
01299 832611

The Shed Factory (summerhouses)
Cambridge
01223 359540

E C Walton & Company Ltd (sheds)
Newark, Nottinghamshire
01636 821215

TOOLS AND EQUIPMENT
Arco Watford (safety equipment)
Watford, Hertfordshire
01923 202090

Bahco Tools Ltd
Halesowen, West Midlands
0121 5045200

Black and Decker
Slough, Berkshire
01753 574277

Bosch Ltd (power tools)
Uxbridge, Middlesex
01895 838791

Ceka Works Ltd
Pwllheli, Gwynedd
01758 701070

Cobra
Atlas Copco Construction and
Mining Ltd
Hemel Hempstead, Hertfordshire
01442 222296

J B Corrie and Co Ltd (wheelbarrows)
Petersfield, Hampshire
01730 262552

Darlac Products (garden tools)
Slough, Berkshire
01753 547790

DEWalt (power tools)
Slough, Berkshire
01753 567055

E-Z Up (canvas shelter)
Houten, The Netherlands
(31) 30 6354100

Faulks & Co (Tubtrugs – flexible buckets)
Nuneaton, Warwickshire
02476 388600

Felco (secateurs and pruning equipment)
Leicester
0116 2344644

Greenbrook Electrical Plc
(powerbreakers)
Harlow, Essex
01279 772700

Honda UK (mowers and rotavators)
Chiswick, London
01753 590500

Husqvarna Forest and Garden UK
(chainsaws and safety clothing)
Stonehouse, Gloucestershire
01453 820310

ITW Construction Products
Swansea
01792 589800

Midland Power Machinery
(turf-stripping machines)
Worcester
01905 763027

SBN Tools Limited (hire, sales, repairs)
Leyton, London
020 8556 5544

SGB Youngman (ladders)
Maldon, Essex
01621 855855

Spear and Jackson (forks and spades)
Sheffield, South Yorkshire
0114 2814242

Wacker (Great Britain) Ltd (wacker plates)
Waltham Cross, Hertfordshire
01992 707222

Wolf Garden Ltd
Tredegar, Blaenau Gwent
01495 306600

WATER
Gardena (irrigation and hosepipes)
Baldock, Hertfordshire
0191 2171537

Good Directions Ltd (accessories)
Southampton, Hampshire
01489 577828

Hozelock Ltd (hozepipe and fittings)
Aylesbury, Buckinghamshire
01844 291881

Interpet (water pumps)
Dorking, Surrey
01306 873818 (for local stockists)

Mill Water Gardens Ltd
Romsey, Hampshire
01794 513444

Oase (UK) Ltd (water pumps, lights, etc.)
Andover, Hampshire
01264 333225

Solar Solutions Fountains (solar pumps)
Kington, Herefordshire
01544 230303

Silverland Stone Ltd (slate water features)
Chertsey, Surrey
01932 569277

Stuart Turner Ltd (pumps)
Henley-on-Thames, Oxfordshire
01491 572655

WOOD PRODUCTS
ATF Supplies (fencing materials)
Andover, Hampshire
01264 366211

Peter Bond (hazel hurdles and arches)
Fordingbridge, Hampshire
01725 518008

Anthony de Grey Trellises (trellis)
London
Tel: 020 7738 8866

English Hurdle (living willow hedges)
Taunton, Somerset
01823 698418

Frolics Ltd (MDF Trellis)
Warkwickshire
01455 212172

Garden Heritage (garden structures)
Milford on Sea, Hampshire
01590 644799

Jungle Giants (bamboo screens)
Tenbury Wells, Worcestershire
01584 819885 (for appointments)

Qual Craft Ltd (oak-weave screening)
Presteigne, Powys
01544 260033

Rusticraft (rustic arbour and trellis)
Lincoln
01522 721014

Terrace and Garden Ltd
(gazebos, vine trellis, galvanized pots)
Bishop's Stortford, Hertfordshire
01799 543289

Thatch International Ltd
(split-screen fencing)
Stockbridge, Hampshire
0845 6009292

Touchwood European Ltd
(willow panels, copper/wood planters)
Hanworth, Norfolk
01263 761717

Trackwork Ltd (railway sleepers)
Doncaster, South Yorkshire
01302 365222

Weaver Plant Ltd (railway sleepers)
Bristol
01761 452391

Picture credits

BBC Worldwide would like to thank the following for providing photographs and for permission to reproduce copyright material. While every effort has been made to trace and acknowledge all copyright holders, we would like to apologize should there have been any errors or omissions.

BBC Worldwide/Susan Bell 2, 4, 5, 7, 8, 9, 10, 11, 12, 13, 14, 15b, 16, 17, 18, 19, 20, 21, 22, 23, 24, 27t, 28, 30, 31, 32, 33t, 36, 37, 38, 39, 40, 41, 42t 43, 44, 45, 46, 49, 53, 54, 55, 57, 58, 59, 60, 61, 65b, 66, 72, 73t, 75, 78t, 80, 81, 84, 85, 86, 87, 88, 89, 90, 91, 93, 94, 95, 96, 97b, 98, 99, 100, 101, 102, 103, 105, 106, 107, 113, 115, 116, 117, 118, 119, 120, 121, 122, 123, 124, 125, 126, 127, 128, 129, 130, 131, 132, 133, 134, 135, 136, 137, 140, 141, 142, 143, 144, 145, 146, 147, 148, 150, 151b, 153, 155; *BBC Gardener's World Magazine/*Tim Sandall 47; **BBC Worldwide/John Glover** 79, 104, 112; **/Tim Sandall** 15t, 25, 27b, 33b, 35, 42b, 48, 67, 78b, 111b, 138, 152; **/Jo Whitworth** 56l, 56c, 62l, 62c, 62r, 73bl, 73bc, 73br, 97t, 109r; **Jonathan Buckley** 77; **Garden & Wildlife Matters** 26, 50, 52, 64, 65t, 69, 109c; **Garden Picture Library** 68 **(Howard Rice)**, 70l, 82 **(John Glover)**, 70c **(Juliette Wade)**, 70r **(Didier Willery)**, 71 **(Brian Carter)**, 74 **(Howard Rice)**, 76, 135 (repeat), 149 **(Mark Bolton)**, 83, 92 **(Friedrich Strauss)** 151t **(Lynne Brotchie)**, 154 **(Sunniva Harte)**,139 **(Michael Howes)**; **Jo Whitworth** 51, 56r, 63, 108, 109l, 110, 111t.

Safety warning

Many of the ideas and projects included in this book involve the use of electrical appliances. Always be aware that using tools incorrectly or without due care can have fatal results, so always read the instructions before you start and make sure you take the proper precautions. The water gardening projects included in this book include electrically powered pumps and every effort has been made to recommend the safest ways of installing them. When you buy electrical components for ponds, always check that they are designed to be used in water and, if in doubt, seek the advice of a qualified electrician. Advice is also given on child safety and every care has been taken to ensure that this information is correct. It should be noted, however, that children can drown in very shallow depths of water and must not be left unsupervised near a water feature. The publishers and the authors cannot accept responsibility or liability for accidents incurred as a result of the construction of any of the projects described in this book.

Index